Entre~~pre~~neurship
MA

**Plain Talk from the CEO who
Learned the Hard Way
What Business Schools
Don't Teach**

Martin J. Geesaman

Dedication

To my partner, my best friend, my soulmate, my wife, Kimberly. Without her love, caring, patience, and tolerance of my constant whining, sniveling and bitching, I would never have made it. She forced me to keep things in perspective and keep my life's priorities straight. Without Kim at my side I would have, at best, given up and, at worst, really given up.

To my staff whose loyalty and dedication and sacrifice have made this enterprise possible and sustainable through good times and bad. They also make ComNav a fun place to work and a joy to be there everyday.

And finally to my reps, vendors, and other business associates who have become close friends. If I had not had their patience, understanding, and confidence in me, ComNav would have ceased to exist on multiple occasions.

Contents

ONE: What It Is and What It Isn't..................11
What Happened to Me . Growing A Company . What This Book is Not

TWO: Important Principles........................41
Your Family Is Your Lifeboat; Don't Let It Sink . Five Core Principles . Ten More Basic Principles

THREE: The Start-Up..............................49
Serendipity . Initial Financing and Vulture Capitalists . Treat Cash as Water in the Desert . Wearing Many Hats

FOUR: The Market 59
Be Careful in Defining Your Market . Expanding the Niche. Find a Market Niche Showing Minimal Competition . Create and Protect Your Brand . Market Products as Broadly as Possible . Your Competitors Are Not Your Enemies

FIVE: Selling Your Products......................72
Sales Reps Exponentially Increase Your Presence . Trade Shows Generally Are Not Worth the Money . Limit Customers' Access to Your Capacity . Make Statements with Your Advertising . Always Do Business on Your Terms, Not Your Customer's Terms . Work with Your Customers, Not for Them

SIX: The Product 79
What We Do . Competitive and Non-competitive Products . The Five Fickle Fingers of Fate . Know Where the Edge of the Cliff Is . Patents Are Scratchier Than Toilet Paper

SEVEN: Your Work Environment and Your Staff.......84
Create a Fun Environment for Your People to Enjoy . Get Good People. Get Them What They Need. Stay Out of Their Way . Rituals, Rewards and Reprimands

EIGHT: External Associates ....…….......99
Your Sales Reps Are Your Face to the Customer . Vendors Are Your Strength . Accountants, Bankers and Lawyers . Weasels and Slicky Boys Are The Enemy . Headhunters, Consultants, Brokers and Other Parasites

NINE: Management ………………………………. 108
Remember You Are the Boss . Learn from Your Mistakes and Let Them Go . Sometimes You Have to Be an Obnoxious Jerk; Other Times It's Just Fun . Pushovers Get Pushed Over . Make Embezzlement As Difficult As Possible . Your Negotiation Strength Is Proportional to What You Are Willing to Lose . Don't Get Too Bogged Down in Details . Take a Motley Moment . Your Primary Job Is Strategic Planning and Conflict Resolution

TEN: The Staff ………......................................116
Wanted: An Open Mind and a Sense of Humor . ComNav's Three-tier Probation Period . In Their Own Words

ELEVEN: The Bottom Line ………......................127
The Plan . Manure Has Several Effects on the Soil System . Immediate Supply of Nutrients . Delayed Supply of Nutrients . Salt and Ammonia Toxicity . Improved Soil Structure . Enhanced Biological Activity . Different Animal Species Produce Different Types of Manure . Retrospective

Introduction

No, the title of this book is not a typo. Typically when starting a company from scratch, all you have is an idea and a dream. You spend months coming up with a rational business plan including sales forecasts, an operational plan, and financial forecasts out to the requisite five years. After you finish your business plan, you step back and look at your handiwork with pride. Now your task is to get other people to believe it, too, even though deep down in your heart you know it is total unadulterated bullshit.

To you it is sweet-smelling manure. Everything in your business plan is based on your research, extrapolation, guesswork and beliefs. Other than your name on the cover, there may not be one cold hard fact in the entire document. It is basically a plan of dreams. Luckily there are people who will invest in dreams as long as they consider them rational. These people are called vulture capitalists. (Actually the real term is venture capitalists, but most are vultures. More on that later.)

My experiences in creating ComNav Engineering started in my basement as a part-time consulting and software company. I began manufacturing when my full-time employer discontinued the product line I was managing. I was able to obtain financing, buy the equipment, retain the customers and create a real company. The company started strong and then almost went under—twice. Then the telecom boom hit and we grew at an exponential rate. Then we crashed at an even faster rate when the tech bubble burst. After being sued and surviving on the backs of my suppliers, I was able to slowly dig out of the hole and grow a sustainable business with a broad customer base.

The term roller-coaster does not even begin to describe the history of ComNav Engineering.

My goal in writing this book is to help all aspiring

entremanures create a fun place to come to work every day, build a sustainable business without slitting their wrists or blowing their heads off during the dark days. I am not joking. If it weren't for my family and the never-ending support of my wife, I would not be here right now. Your company is your identity. It's who you are. So if it fails you feel like a failure yourself. At those times the depths of desperation and depression you experience are almost unbearable.

On the flip side when the customers are happy, production is cruising, and the cash is flowing, the exhilaration is so intense it is hard to sit still. So basically if you decide to become an entremanure, you've decided to live life with a bipolar disorder.

Although ComNav Engineering is an engineering and manufacturing company and most of the advice in these pages is from a manufacturing perspective, the scenarios, events, strategies and business processes are universal. All businesses have investors (even if you are the only one), employees, vendors, customers, and products. All businesses have good days and bad days. All business owners make mistakes. The key to survival and ultimate success is to learn from the not-so-good days and the mistakes and move on. I have always found that it helps to cry on the shoulder of someone who has been there and done that. Hopefully my experiences will help you get through the bad days while maintaining your sense of humor and enable you to move past your mistakes.

1   What It Is and What It Isn't

What Happened to Me

In high school I was a stoner nerd. I do not say this to glorify it, but to show that you do not have to be part of the popular clique, the brainiac, or homecoming king to be an entremanure. Even a stoner can have enough brain cells left over to start and successfully manage a company.

Running a company requires some basic skills. Mostly it requires ambition and enough confidence to trust your gut and the ability to make decisions given minimal facts and then following through. This part of the book may seem a bit self-indulgent, but my background and the experiences that make up my character affect the way I make decisions

There are common characteristics of entremanures and I fit the typical profile: first-born son, worked and had a business as a kid, dislikes authority, values freedom more than security, likes to be self-reliant and not dependent on other people, focuses on the end result of long-term projects, sees the big picture and doesn't get bogged down in the details, has a strong belief in the abilities of other people, is able to delegate tasks and move on, and is goal-oriented. There are other traits but these pretty much describe me in a nutshell. I consider myself the opposite of a type-A personality. It takes a lot to get me rattled and I very rarely lose it. When I do lose it, I don't throw things or lash out at people, I pace my office, hurl a stream of choice verbiage at no one in particular and snort. Snorting is a characteristic of the males in my family and it was source of great entertainment watching my brothers do it when we were growing up. I am very laid back and tend to ostrich problems until the very last minute, in hopes they will solve themselves, just go away, or until I can see all of the possible options available for a solution.

Of all my personality traits this one drives the women in my life nuts: my mother, my first wife, my wife now, and even the women on my staff, including my daughter. It affects the men, too, but for some reason women want problems fixed now, and when I say it's not time to worry about that yet, the stares could cut carbide steel.

My first job at age 14 was at a pig farm. I lasted about a week. It started fine: planting, baling hay, and general farm tasks. At the end of the week I was informed it was time to castrate the male piglets. I got them out of the pen, and the farmer slit the sack, flipped the testicles up in the air and the dog caught them and slurpped them up like a raw oyster. I was dumbfounded. I don't know which was worse: the sound of the piglet squealing, or the sound of the dog slurping up his nuts. I had never seen anything like it. Well after momma heard her first baby squeal, she was not interested in letting me any where near her other kids. So the other boy I was working with, the farmer's son and one of my classmates, came up with a distract-and-grab strategy. One of us got into the pen and jumped around like an idiot, and when momma came after him, the other one grabbed a piglet. Hopefully the distracter could jump out of the pen before 400-pound momma crushed him against the pen wall. Of course this was a source of great entertainment for the farmer. After that first week I decided for the first time in my life it was time for a career change.

In a couple weeks I got a new job as a stock boy at my town's Western Auto store. I bounced around the store taking inventory, sorting out deliveries, sweeping up, helping customers and general everyday store stuff. The store's owner was my first business mentor. He taught me to deal with customers, manage inventories and generally how a small business works. He had a great sense of humor and we laughed a lot. One of the most important things he taught me was to have fun at work. He realized I had decent mechanical skills so he had me assembling bicycles and lawn mowers. Eventually I was actually repairing them as well. I thought, Why not do this on my own? So at age 14 I became a business owner and started my first company: Marty's Bike Repair.

I went to the local stationery store, bought a receipt book, cleaned out a corner of our garage and hung out my shingle. The kids in town stopped by and I adjusted their brakes and gears. I fixed flat tires, and did general maintenance on their bikes. I got parts at Western Auto using my employee discount and then marked them up. I didn't make a lot of money, but I was making a net profit, even though at the time I didn't know what *net* meant. My parents approved of it all because as long as I was in my bike shop, they knew they would not be getting a call to pick me up at the police station.

I had various jobs throughout high school: plant nursery worker, store clerk, janitor, lawn mower, parking lot attendant, gate watchman, gardener, trash collector, car washer. But even then, in spite of the small cash flow, I loved the freedom and flexibility of my little bike shop. I was already realizing I did not like having a boss. None of the people I worked for were mean in any way; I just didn't like to be told what to do.

While in high school I was partying with some friends and the subject of the future came up. We were sitting around talking about things we would like to do before we died (what is now called a bucket list). I have no idea why this conversation stuck with me more than any of the other idiotic ones we had, but I decided to actually achieve the goals that I set for myself. Over the years that list has been added to, but the first five put me on the path of always having goals and working toward them. They were not really profound goals and some were actually stupid. But, hey, I was a teenage kid. What did I know?

These goals were:
1. Drive across country in a van. (It was the 70s.)
2. Take my kids to Disney World at the perfect age: between five and twelve. (My family never took us. It had just been built.)
3. Make love in a gondola in Venice. (I was a romantic.)
4. Start my own company. (I had no idea what.)
5. Go camping in the mountains in Peru to see if aliens came. (I told you I was a stoner nerd!)

Only one of these goals has not yet been accomplished: the trip to Peru. Notice how vague they are. I have always made my goals very generic. I figured I would fill in the details when the time arrived. My current goal (and the one that got me through the dark days of the Telecom crash), is my goal of retiring with my wife on a sailboat. Obviously a boat big enough for both of us to live on is of considerable size and expense. I have pretty much taken the attitude that Com-Nav Engineering is my only avenue to acquire enough cash to get the boat, outfit it, and retire on it. Though a couple of times I was willing to give up the dream to escape the nightmare, I always came back after a short time and said, "Damn it, I want that boat! I want to sail. I want pristine palm tree lagoons and tropical sun. I like watching my wife sunbathe topless on the beach. I cannot give up!" My goals gave me strength and a second wind. Goals can be powerful motivators and give a person the strength to get through extremely hard times.

When I completed high school I had no idea what I was going to do. On any given day my career aspirations ran the gamut from photographer to doctor. I went to college assuming that was what I was supposed to do. It was a total waste of my parents' money, but I had a great time! At the end of my first semester I had a G.P.A of 0.5. Obviously I needed to look at other career opportunities. I left for Navy boot camp in Orlando, Florida, that April in 1977. Apparently I was not the only one with this problem. The kid who played Dennis the Menace on TV graduated a few months before I got there.

The Navy changed my life and gave me purpose. I learned discipline, responsibility, the strength of true friendship and, most importantly, a career goal. I had aced the standard test they gave, and the recruiter was trying to score bonus points by having me go nuke and be a submariner. I thought about it, at first thinking it would be cool to be on a submarine—probably the closest I would ever get to living like I was on Star Trek. But the previous September our neighbor, who was a few years older than me, came home on a visit after being on a six-month deployment. It was the first time he had seen the sun in six months, and while everyone else had at least some color to them, he looked like an albino. I took a good look at myself and decided I would most likely get claustrophobic and probably freak out. So I signed up as an Aviation Electronic Tech. I figured at least I could play Frisbee on the deck of an aircraft carrier.

After the Navy I went to work as a tech at K&L Microwave. At the time I didn't even know what a filter was. I actually thought I was going to help manufacture microwave ovens. K&L was, and arguably still is, the industry leader for filter manufacturers. There are some bigger Japanese companies but they are concentrated in specific markets and make large volumes of a few different parts, but K&L is the largest supplier that tries to fit every market with a broad range of products. I initially worked for a year as a production tuner. I was good at it and quickly learned to prototype a broad range of products.

After about eight months I was bored so I talked to a small marine electronics company, thinking that working on boats could be fun. The owner told me that with my Navy training I had the skills, but I needed an FCC license with a radar endorsement before he could hire me. I went to the library, checked out a study guide, and studied every night after work for three months. Then I went back to the owner with my freshly printed FCC license with a radar endorsement in hand. It sounds like a major accomplishment, but other than learning how tubes work; it was basically a refresher course.

> **SCAR WARS: Battle #1**
> It was during this period I got my first really bad hit. I was on top of a clam dredger tuning a radar. The magnetron is extremely sensitive and you are not supposed to touch it with another piece of metal. My screwdriver slipped and in order to avoid whacking the magnetron, I jumped and it went right into the high voltage box. Of course the boat (including the top of the cabin where I was standing), was made of metal. My legs went into spasms and straightened up so fast that I went flying. The top of a clam dredger cabin is a good 30 to 40 feet in the air. If my arm had not become tangled in the rigging, I would have really screwed myself up.

During the spring and summer we were very busy. At times it was hot and nasty work, crawling around the bilges of fishing boats and climbing masts. (Did I mention I am afraid of heights?)

It was late fall; it was getting cold; and since it was off-season, I was getting bored again. My boss, a retired RCA engineer, had been telling me for a couple of weeks that I had what it took to be an engineer and that I should go for it. The night I took that hit, I had an existential moment. I don't know if it was feeling the lack of direction, the dead-end jobs I saw ahead of me, or the 10,000 volts that just nailed my butt, but I got depressed to the point of actually crying. I wanted to go back to college and try to get through engineering school, but I had no idea where to begin. Since my last college experience was, shall we say, less than glorious, I assumed the registrar would just laugh me out of his office. My wife was very supportive and said if this was what I really wanted to do and I would stay focused, she would get a couple of jobs if she had to in order to help with the bills. I thought we just might be able to make it work.

It was about this time K&L called me and asked if I wanted to come back. They were growing and could not find the techs they needed. K&L also had an education program to help with tuition. I went back to K&L and also talked to the registrar at the local college. K&L surprised me by giving me a decent raise and the college allowed me to sign up for classes on a probationary basis. They had a dual degree program with the University of Maryland and if I got decent grades in my first two semesters I could be admitted into the program. In the end I did not use K&L's education benefit. I found other avenues because their program came with too many strings attached (understandable, given the cost of college). About this same time I saw in the paper that a new TV station was starting up. I had an FCC license, so on a whim I filled out an application, and then soon forgot about it.

Eleven months and three weeks later, I took a week's vacation. (The timing was significant. More about that later.) We weren't planning on going anywhere because with school bills, cash was tight. Before I left work one of my coworkers said a man who used to work there was trying to get in touch with me. I had no idea who this man was, and I was about to start a week of partying, hanging out at the beach, and doing some fishing, so I could not have cared less. As soon as I walked through the door of my house, the phone rang. The man on the phone told me his name but I had never heard of him before. I learned he was the chief engineer at

the new TV station. He had been looking through the files, came across my application, and wanted to talk to me.
I asked, "Okay, when?" He said, "What are you doing now?" I went. The man looked like a reject from a Hell's Angels' convention: big build, long hair, scraggly beard.
"You Marty Geesaman?" he asked.
"Yeah."
"You get high?" he asked.
After a doobie and a couple shots of Drambuie at the bar around the corner, I began my broadcast career.

It turned out the ex-K&L employee who was trying to contact me also worked at that TV station. They had both found my application and wanted to see if I was interested in the job. The story was that the family that opened the station blew through their start-up cash and the station was in receivership. Their son was the chief engineer and was no longer allowed on the property. They needed someone to run the transmitter and help out with the studio equipment. I took the job and essentially went on vacation from K&L. I never went back. That turned out to be a bad move on my part. When I went to get my vacation paycheck, they said I had to work there a year to get vacation time. I argued that, including vacation, I was there a year. They said vacation didn't count. (Were they being slimy? Yes, but looking back I screwed them, too. Now someone else had to pick up my slack.) I went to the president's office and lost it. I cut loose a temper tantrum that amazed even me. Some of the things said make me cringe to this day. If I had been that man, I would have punched me out.

The reason I am going into this much detail about these events is to illustrate a point: *It is not good business to hold grudges.* I had learned a lot about business in general, and the filter industry in particular, during my earlier years at K&L. I have also incorporated some of their rituals and business practices into my own company.

About a year after this incident, the TV station's

microwave link between the studio and transmitter was acting up and I thought it might have shifted frequency. I called K&L and asked if I could borrow a microwave frequency counter to test it and the president agreed. I don't remember if I apologized or not. I probably did but he didn't hold a grudge. Actually I think he got his satisfaction by seeing my temper tantrum and he just moved on. Bottom line: I let them down and I deserved what I got. I later went back and worked at K&L three more times, both before and after earning my engineering degree. I worked at the TV station for about three years. It was a great job for a college student. Routine maintenance does not take that much time and if you keep the equipment up to par, emergencies are rare. So there is a lot of time spent just sitting around. I pretty much did all my homework at work. My boss didn't care as long as when I was needed I immediately dropped the books and fixed the problem.

During this time I took my second big hit, though technically I didn't actually get shocked that time. But I almost broke both arms. The transmitter kept overheating and I knew it was because the contactors for the fans were undersized and kept melting. We had been planning on replacing them on the next overnight, but out of four contactors, two had already melted and the third just went. If the transmitter overheated it could ruin our $50,000 klystron. The smart thing to do would have been to wait until we went off the air, shut down all the power and changed the contactor. But no. I figured if I was careful and took someone with me I could do it hot. I did not want to go out to the transmitter by myself in the middle of the night. I would much rather have been home in bed, especially since I had an exam the next day.

We had an employee in the production department who also did odd jobs around the station when someone needed muscle. He went by the name of Dancing Bear. I asked Bear if he would go out to the transmitter with me. As his name implies, Dancing Bear was a big dude. He was also a great, salt-of-the-earth, good soul, an easygoing type of person. We went out to the transmitter, about 15 miles out of town in the woods. When we got there I gave him a broom, told him what I was going to do, and told him that if he saw sparks he should knock me off the power with the broom handle. He said "Geese, I don't want to hit you!" Being somewhat dramatic, I told him he could either knock me off or smell me cooking. He agreed and stood over me like a batter at home plate.

I probably don't have to tell you what happened next. Sure enough the screws were tight; the screwdriver slipped, shorting out two terminals and sparks flew. Luckily I jumped back just as Bear was coming down with all his strength right where my arms had been. After a minute of heavy breathing, we looked at each other and busted a gut laughing.

It was around this time that I started ComNav (the first time). The college I was attending had a small TV studio and they had the same brand of equipment we had at the TV station. I was very familiar with the equipment, so they hired me as a consultant to maintain their studio. They eventually acquired more equipment and needed someone full time. They offered me the job.

I still had about two years to finish up the first part of my degree before I had to move up to College Park to attend the University of Maryland. I told them that was my intention and they were fine with it. The biggest perk was that since I would be a fulltime employee of the college I would get free tuition. SCORE! I took the job. This time though I gave two weeks' notice to the TV station. I had decided that burning bridges is not a good idea.

I was working at the college, taking classes, and consulting on the side. I worked on boats, college language labs, radio stations, and made custom cables for a friend's rock band. I even worked on a commercial microwave oven for a company that fried bacon for the army. It was during this period that I took <u>my third big hit</u>.

> ## SCAR WARS: Battle #2
>
> One of my clients was an AM radio station. Their transmitter interlock kept popping and taking them off the air. I went out to the transmitter at night after they signed off to run some tests. I went alone. (Can you say dumb ass?) I had the current sensor from the antenna in my hand and balanced a scope probe on the center contact and slowly turned up the modulation. The interlock kicked out with a loud bang. It startled me and the probe slipped and hit the palm of my hand. Of course my other hand was braced on the side of the metal transmitter cabinet. I took it right across the chest. My legs snapped again and I went flying a good 20 feet out of the transmitter room and landed under the workbench in the workroom. I think I was unconscious for about 30 minutes. It took about a week for my head to completely clear. Luckily there was no permanent damage (though some people may disagree).

The next few years were devoted to moving to College Park and finishing up my degree at the University of Maryland. The problem with the dual-degree program is that by the time a person gets to College Park, all that remains are the pure engineering classes. I barely slept the entire time. But I did make it through with a decent GPA. During that first semester my son was born. I was a full-time student, unemployed, with a wife and baby. Thankfully my parents helped by letting my wife and son stay with them while I was in school.

That first summer I went back to K&L and took a temporary job tuning filters as a technician. I had been there a couple of weeks when an old friend called. He had started at K&L within a week of when I did the first time I worked there. He was working at the company K&L had spun out of in a town about 12 miles from College Park and asked if I would come up and work for him. This would allow me to make some decent bucks, set up an apartment, and move my family back with me. I took the job and this time I gave two weeks' notice. Since I was a temp they said not to worry about it, so I only stayed another week. I got up to Cir-Q-Tel and took the engineering job. Even though I wasn't finished earning my degree yet, they determined I was close enough and had enough experience to be hired as an engineering assistant and they agreed to give me time off for school.

The man who owned Cir-Q-Tel was a pioneer in the industry. His was one of the first microwave filter companies and he had developed most of the products and processes all the other companies were using. But he was an engineer, not a businessman. They occasionally landed a big contract, but for the most part they were always hanging on by their fingernails. They had already filed chapter 11 bankruptcy two or three times and were on their way to filing another time. There were already five or more companies that could directly trace their lineage to Cir-Q-Tel. Engineers worked there for a few years and then left to start their own companies. The owner just did not want to grow. He could not delegate, micro-managed every detail and essentially drove us all nuts. But on his good days he was a great man and was fun to be around.

I worked there until I finished my degree and due to the chaos of the environment, I had no intention of sticking around. The friend who had hired me was already long gone. But all in all, it was a good experience, allowing me to be with my family while finishing school. I also learned a great deal about the industry as well as some things not to do.

From the time I was a little kid, my dream job had been to work for NASA. During the Mercury flights I used to sit in front of our black and white TV with a big fish bowl on my head, pretending I was an astronaut. During my last semester at the University of Maryland, I peppered the world with my resume. Amazingly NASA sent me a response. It was for their tracking station at Wallops Island, Virginia, about 20 miles from my hometown.

When I was very young my family had always driven through Wallops on our way to the beach at Assateague. I stared at the huge antennas and wondered what they were focused on. I had an interview and now I would be working around that same huge antenna farm.

The job consisted of maintaining and upgrading their tracking radars and some operations work during shuttle flights when they resumed. (The *Challenger* explosion had been the year before). The interview was a success; I got the job offer. And then K&L called and offered me double the salary. I went back and forth but eventually greed trumped childhood dreams. Ten, twenty, maybe even thirty percent, but double? I had a family by then and another baby on the way, so I could not afford to be idealistic.

I worked at K&L for another three years. Technically I was loving life. I bounced around different areas of the company as the product engineer for miniature filters, cavities, and multiplexers, switched filter banks and integrated assemblies. By this time K&L had become a completely vertically integrated company. We had our own board shop, plating lab, machine shop, environmental test lab, and custom capacitor cutting. Technically working there was an engineer's wet dream.

This was when I discovered office politics. Up to this point in my career I had not worked in a staff position. It was somewhat of a staff job at Cir-Q-Tel, but that place was run as a fiefdom, so there was little room for politics. There were some major egos in K&L's engineering department, mine included. There was a lot of backstabbing and taking credit for other people's work. I was constantly getting into trouble because I had a problem keeping my mouth shut. After a while I knew the writing was on the wall and I had a feeling that I either already was (or soon would be), the target of a set-up.

About that time I received a call from a headhunter. As it happened someone with an MBA had bought out Cir-Q-Tel from its most recent bankruptcy and he needed to beef up his engineering staff. We met and he offered me the position of Director of Engineering and 10% of the company. I accepted, packed up the family and moved back to D.C.

The bulk of my business education came from Cir-Q-Tel. The first few months I was there we were all full of anticipation. The company had a good base business, and we had a decent engineer, (named Marty Geesaman), and a decent salesman. We figured we could only go up. We soon learned that the man who had bought the company had less than zero knowledge of the industry. I first started noticing something out of line when he flew all our sales representatives to Santa Fe, New Mexico, for a sales/ training meeting. He paid all the airfare, rented two adjoining villas, and gave everyone expensive artistic ceramic tiles. I figured he must have been sitting on a lot of cash.

How wrong could I be? He was leveraging everything.

Then he started selling products even though he had no clue of their cost, complexity, or our ability to manufacture them. His goal was to build the backlog; it didn't matter if we could make money on it, or even if we could actually build it. He was running a pyramid scheme that would show the bankers backlog and then he borrowed against it. Once I realized what was going on I returned my stock to him. The company was set up as an S-Corp and I didn't want anything to do with it. The pyramid eventually collapsed and the bank sold the company out from under him. The IRS also went after him for not paying payroll taxes. Thank God I had given my stock back! Every payday saw us all race to the bank, because the last one there had a rubber check. Time for a career change, again, so I peppered the world with my resume.

That man actually made me lose it a few times and I am still embarrassed on occasion about how I treated him in the end. In fact at one point over Christmas he was trying to make nice and bought me a bottle of Drambuie for a present. Given his state of mind and the way I was acting, I opened it in his office poured both of us a glass. I actually waited for him to drink first thinking he may be trying to poison me. Yes, I know that was probably paranoid in the extreme, but I didn't trust him and I sure as hell wasn't going to unnecessarily pour out good Drambuie. (I really like Drambuie!) But I swear, if you gave the man a gram of sympathy or compassion, he turned it into a full-fledged guilt trip about how everything was everyone else's fault. I have never met a more delusional person in my life.

But I do owe him a significant amount of praise in teaching me many, many things *not* to do when running my own company.

During my time at the University of Maryland, a lot of my classmates and I wanted to get jobs at Hughes Aircraft Company. Hughes was on the forefront of everything. They were doing the coolest, most high-tech military stuff. Never in my wildest dreams did I think I could get a job at Hughes. But I did.

I love to program and at that time I was writing a program to design filters. Basically I designed something once, figured out the process and then programmed it so the next time I could do it by just entering some data and hitting a couple of keys. It has been said that the best engineers are the laziest people. If that is true then I am one hell of an engineer! Windows had not been introduced to the market yet, so most of the world was working in DOS. I had been impressed by the Macintosh operating system, so I wrote a framework for my program in C++ that was pseudo-*Windows* based. The people from the lab at Hughes who interviewed me were looking for an engineer programmer to integrate software and hardware. I showed them my program and they made me an offer.

To be honest I had a blast there. The projects I worked on were fun, challenging, and there was very little supervision. What supervision I did have usually consisted of playful arguments with my boss over whether C++ or Visual Basic was faster, easier, and made smaller programs, or the occasional code contest. (I still have these same arguments today with my son.) The engineers and scientists in our lab met once or twice a week, divvied up tasks, and then met again a couple of days later to compare notes and integrate our work. It was great. But it was not to last.

This took place around the time the Berlin Wall came down and the Cold War ended. Our lab was being shut down and I was soon to be laid off with 20,000 other people from Hughes Aircraft Company. Again I was looking for a job.

GTE Control Devices found me through a headhunter. I had never been to Maine, but the opportunity sounded like fun. I would have a lot of independence since I was the only RF engineer there among a group of top ceramic engineers and nobody else would know what I was doing.

In 1992 I moved my family to Maine and took the job at GTE Control Devices. GTE had a huge ceramic plant that used to make PTC carburetor heaters. When the automotive industry switched to fuel injection, that business disappeared overnight. So they went for years with cobwebs growing in their kilns. Then in the late 80s microwave ceramics started to hit the market in cellular base stations and other applications in large numbers. It turned out that PTCs were much more difficult to produce than the dielectric ceramics used in the microwave market. I think it was during a trade show that a man from Allen Telecom and another man from GTE were drinking in a bar one night. The Allen Telecom man was complaining about how difficult it was to get the dielectrics he needed from Japan. The GTE man mentioned they had an idle ceramic plant up in Maine and suggested a meeting with a man from GTE labs to see if they could put something together. They met; the technology fit; and in six months Control Devices was making top-quality ceramics. But there was a problem. They had excellent ceramic engineers and they were making top quality parts, but they did not have an electrical engineer on staff to do the application work. Who were the customers? What are the applications? Where does it fit in the system? How can testing be standardized? What is the market price? That's why they came looking for someone with my training and background.

Once I got there I asked if I could start up a coaxial filter group to make filters out of our ceramics. It was totally new technology and I would have a chance to do something brand new. Management told me to write up a plan and if it looked reasonable they would fund it. I did; they did; and that is how I got into the ceramic filter business.

I hired an intern from the University of Maine and we had three years of interrupted time to play in the lab. We tried different coating techniques, various filter structures, different coupling mechanisms, different package styles, production techniques—basically all the raw research to start a filter product line from scratch.

By the second year we found a couple of customers who focused our efforts on real products to be produced rather than being just a couple of nerds playing with our belly button lint in the lab. By the third year were able to produce hundreds and then thousands of very high-spec filters. Doing this research in a high volume automotive company forced me to change my previous filter-manufacturing paradigm. It forced us to come up with high-volume production techniques that were new to the microwave filter industry, which usually builds things one at a time.

Eventually the filter group became too big and the market volatility of the electronics industry did not sit too well with my automotive peers. They were used to sales forecasts that actually were fact, not just speculation. In addition our production process was somewhat messy and the culture of GTE was to keep the place so clean you could eat off the floor. The customers were in a completely different market and they had to make a choice between creating an entirely separate marketing group or shutting it down and bailing out.

They could not just shut it down, because my little filter group had a couple of big customers; one was also one of the company's biggest dielectric customers. They decided to shut down the line. I would be laid off; but I could buy the equipment and go off on my own. They essentially helped me set up my company and I took the liability off their shoulders so they didn't have to worry about being sued. That was now *my* problem.

Up to now I had been working on an MBA and doing side consulting jobs, as well as designing and occasionally building filters in my basement. Lee Perry, who ran an ad agency in Portland and produced all Control Devices' brochures and marketing materials, occasionally factored my consulting jobs.

Lee and I had met a few years earlier doing the brochures and marketing materials for my filter group. We had hit it off immediately and became fast friends. Up to this point we had toyed with the idea of starting a filter company with Lee providing the backing. He had made money every time he factored me, so he was intrigued by the microwave filter business. GTE Control Devices' decision to shut down the product line had not come as a shock. The writing had been on the wall and I had been expecting it for a few months. I still remember Lee's exact words when I called and told him the news: "How much do you need and when do you need it?"

Growing A Company

ComNav Engineering was first established in 1982 as a technical service hobby company. I bought some military surplus test equipment at a HAM-fest and built a couple of Heath kits and set up a test lab in my basement. The focus of the company at that time was to provide contract-engineering services to the broadcast and fishing industries and pretty much anybody else who came along. Typical work included antenna pattern measurements, installation and service of communication and navigation equipment on fishing boats, repair of commercial microwave ovens used to fry bacon, service a high school language lab and a college TV studio. After spending the day crawling around the bilge of a fishing boat and being covered with bilge slime and then doing an AM radio pattern measurement and being chased by a psychotic, man-eating goose in the same day, I determined that wasn't working for me and I temporarily ceased operations in 1985.

The company started up again in 1987 after I completed work on my electrical engineering degree. The focus was on microwave filters, software design, consulting, occasional CAD, and job shop work. At the beginning I operated the company as a sole proprietorship providing engineering consulting services to several microwave filter companies. My first manufacturing job was actually forced upon me. I had done a full design package for a customer consisting of electrical design, mechanical design, bill of materials, and a full set of assembly drawings. The customer liked what I did and said, "Okay, we want 100 of them." I told them I didn't have the facilities to build the parts but they were insistent. They asked how much I needed and to include the cost of the equipment in the price. So I ran some numbers and came up with a total job cost and divided by 100, plus the tooling costs as a separate line item. That night I had dinner with my friend Lee and told him about it and he asked what my costs would be. I told him and he offered to lend it to me at 1% per month. I thought the customer wouldn't go for it, but I sent a quote anyway. I had a purchase order the next day.

My son (10), daughter (8), and Lee helped me wind coils. I reflow soldered the parts in my wife's Kenmore oven, and tuned the parts at work on the weekends, when the equipment wasn't being used. Since we made ceramic filters at work and these were chip and wire, and it was only a one-shot deal, there was no conflict and my boss said he didn't mind. I still have a couple of those first parts lying around somewhere. It turned out my daughter was very good at hand-soldering coils.

When all the dust settled, I was able to pay Lee back. I had some of the manufacturing equipment left in my basement, and a couple thousand bucks in my pocket. ComNav had become a manufacturing company.

Also during this time my design program was growing into a real engineering CAD package named Filtroid. Around 1993 Filtroid was finished to the point where it was a marketable product. I called my buddy Lee and we produced a brochure and placed a couple of ads. Initially I tried to sell it for $2,900 a copy. No sales. Then $2495. Still nothing. Then $1995. Still nothing. By this point I was getting extremely frustrated. Eventually I settled on a price of $995 and

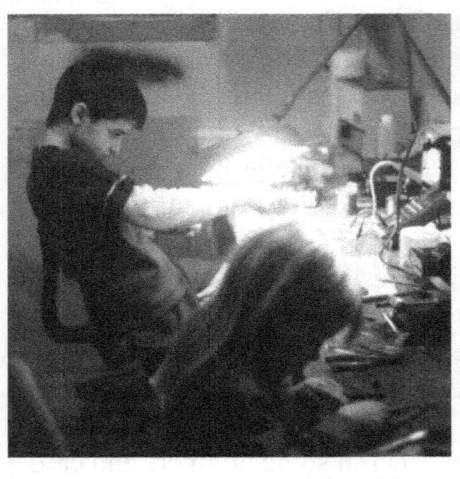

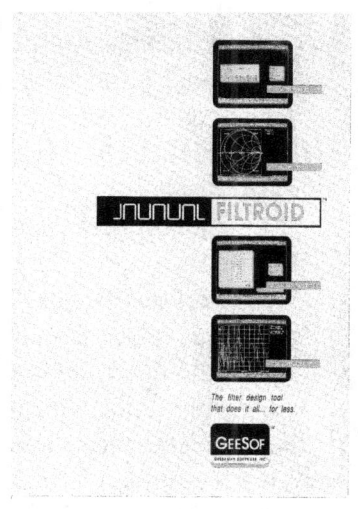

started selling an average of two Filtroids a month. What do you know? Micro-economics works. Once you find the price acceptable to the market, you can get on a supply and demand curve. Not great but my expenses were low for the manual, shipping materials, and hardware key. I had about $200 in cost for each copy sold, plus the cost of occasional ads. Not great but a $795 margin was more than enough to pay my Coors Lite bill. The internet wasn't ubiquitous yet or I probably would have done a lot better with a web page. It was never going to be more than a basement operation anyway.

In 1994 when marketing efforts for Filtroid began, I incorporated the company as a C-Corp in the state of Maine. I choose a C-Corp due to my experience at Cir-Q-Tel. I wanted as big a financial wall between me and my company as possible. Paranoid? Yes but I didn't know what the future held and it's a pain in the butt to change. I later sold the rights to Filtroid to Ansoft for $50,000 and five chairs of their design suite. It has since been incorporated into their Serenade program. I used the money to bail ComNav out during one of the slowdowns.

Through my consulting activity, using my kids as labor (Hey, they wanted to help daddy!), and software sales, ComNav was steadily developing a reputation for innovative design techniques and creating many contacts throughout the microwave industry.

The impetus for the company to begin manufacturing operations full time was the spinoff of Control Devices coaxial filter product line. This event provided ComNav Engineering with a ready-made backlog of business with established customers. Two customers to be exact, but big customers.

The biggest was Metricom and they were nervous because no one else could make the filter I was supplying, and they had redesigned their radio around my part. If GTE had shut down completely and cut them off, the lawyers would have had a field day. So in order to help Lee and me get our financing together, they gave us a $100,000 purchase order for 2000 filters.

I can't really give an accurate picture of ComNav's history without discussing Metricom. For the first five years, our businesses were tightly intertwined and they were our biggest customer. We were essentially Metricom's butt boy, and when they coughed, we came close to respiratory failure. Metricom was established in the wireless remote meter reading business. At one point they invented a spread spectrum technique to jam a lot of data though a narrow bandwidth, and went into the wireless internet business. They were involved in field trials when I met them while working at GTE, and were having problems with system reliability. They did a site survey and installed a radio with minimal filtering using a $2 popcorn filter. Then some man in the neighborhood got a new garage door opener and it jammed their radio. Then they had to climb the pole and install an expensive cavity supplied by one of my competitors. This is a very simplistic explanation of their problem, but it gets the point across.

They were looking for an inexpensive, high performance

filter and they told me if I could make a filter with their specs for under $50, they would redesign their radios to incorporate it. Given where we were in our research, we needed an actual product and I felt confident that we could do it, given some of the techniques we had just developed. Since we were the new kids on the block, they were leery of giving us an order since they never heard of us before, so I took it on as a bet. If I made an acceptable part, they would pay me $5,000 and if I couldn't, they would pay nothing. I got my butt chewed back home at GTE. They were a Fortune 500 company and they didn't do business on a handshake and a bet. To make a long story short, that $5,000 was spent on getting me the first Pentium computer in the company.

When ComNav split off from GTE, Metricom was getting ready to go into production (the first time) with their pole top radios, with my filter as an integral part. When I called them and told them that GTE was shutting the filter group down, they freaked out. The operations manager said he was flying out for a meeting to discuss the situation. I had to show him something to calm him down.

I spent the next few days looking all over Portland for manufacturing space. I found a location and signed a lease. I went directly from the real estate office to the airport to pick up the man from Metricom. I had set up a meeting with the general manager of GTE Control Devices, my partner Lee, and the Metricom man and showed him our filter group, which was still running at GTE.

The general manager of GTE Control Devices assured the Metricom rep that they would do what they could to ease the transition and they were not just going to kick me to the curb. After that meeting I took him to see my new factory. There was nothing in it, just open space. I told him the equipment was on its way (some of it was), and I walked him through the empty shell pointing out where engineering was going to be, where production would be done, where the test lab was going and other interesting details. It didn't take long; it was only 3500 square feet.

That evening Lee met us at a local restaurant and we stuffed ourselves with fresh Maine lobster. One thing I have learned about people from California: If you stuff them full of lobster, negotiations go a lot smoother. We came up with a plan, and Metricom placed the order with ComNav Engineering instead of GTE. There were a couple of bumps along the way but we pulled it off to everyone's satisfaction.

Over the next five years Metricom repeatedly started production, stopped, redesigned their system, started again, stopped, did another upgrade, and then it exploded. Each time they stopped to redesign or upgrade their system, it almost killed us at ComNav. The technology was moving so fast; they just could not get ahead of it. We were scrambling to broaden our customer base, but given the typical three years it takes to go from concept to production on a new system, it was not happening fast enough to stabilize our business. So we were pretty much at Metricom's mercy. If they coughed we almost had respiratory failure. Thank God I had the opportunity to sell my design software Filtroid to Ansoft when I did, or we might have crashed and burned at that point.

When the Telecom boom hit, Metricom had about $1 billion in venture capital from such sources as Paul Allen of Microsoft fame, MCI and Intel. Right before it hit we were suffering from the previous Metricom shutdown and had shrunk to eight people from a peak of 22, were doing about $60K per month in sales and holding on by our fingernails. Then Metricom called and said they needed 20,000 pole-top filters a month and 200 base station filters a month, starting tomorrow. (They were being facetious about tomorrow, but they wanted them fast.)

    I flew out to California and we negotiated a production plan, an initial order, and prepayments to cover our start-up costs. A week later we received two $500,000 checks as prepayments for both the pole-top and cavity filters. This all occurred in September of 1999. By February of 2000 we had opened up another plant and were about 50% of the way toward meeting their production goals. By June we were up to 80 people and meeting their goals of 20,000 pole-tops and 200 base station filters per month. Cash was flowing; things were running smoothly; other big customers were coming on line. We were shipping $1.6 million of product a month. Times were good. Then the bottom fell out.

    Right before the crash we were still growing and had outgrown both our original plant and the newer, larger production facility. I started looking around for more space so I could put the company back together and have everyone in one location. I found an abandoned ice cream plant that was in the process of being refurbished. They had just started and didn't have any fixed plans to build it out. The owner told me he "had to build something, so give me your drawings and we will build that." I had already spent around $150,000 fixing up and modifying our current production plant; now I had to walk away from that investment. That money was spent and not coming back and we needed more space. I ended up spending close to $400,000 on the ice cream plant with custom wiring, environmental controls, security systems, office build-outs and all that goes with customizing a new space.

    This new plant was about 75% done when Metricom got into trouble. I called a staff meeting and asked everyone's opinion on what we should do. After listening to everyone's thoughts, I agreed that Metricom was only one customer; we had others, and more would come on line. I thought Metricom

ice cream plant

was an aberration and there was no way it could affect the entire market. I have never been so wrong in my life.

Within three months after moving into the ice cream plant, five of our largest customers went out of business. Most of them didn't just shut down or go into receivership; they went straight to Chapter 7 liquidation. If it weren't for our terms containing prepayments and cancellation charges we might have joined them immediately. At this point our ship was sinking and we had to chuck everything and everyone overboard to stay afloat. The staff went from 80 to 6 and we moved back to our original 3,500 square-foot plant. Luckily the previous tenant after us had moved out and all our piping and wiring were still in place and we had a month-to-month lease on the ice cream plant.

At this point I just wanted out; I wanted to run away, leave it all and maybe buy a steamer cart and sell hot dogs downtown. My goals and dreams of retiring with my wife on a good-sized sailboat seemed so far away, it seemed ridiculous that I had ever entertained such thoughts. I didn't know where to turn. I actually picked up the phone and dialed six of the ten numbers of one of my competitors and would have sold them everything just to get out from under the debt, and screw the dream. As I was punching the seventh number, my vice president walked in and wanted help with something in the lab. I went with him, played in the lab a little while and calmed down.

Over the next two years business slowly improved to the point where we could just barely hang on. But my payables were getting pushed out so big and so far, I expected to come to work any day and see yellow tape on the door. We sprinkled a little cash to everyone every month. Not enough even to stay current, but to let them know that we might be on life support, but we weren't dead yet. I thank God for my vendors to this day. Because of their patience and understanding we are still here. Any one of them could have pulled me under. <u>But they didn't</u> want to see me go into bankruptcy and settle for pennies on the dollar. They were willing to take the risk and see if I could do it.

It was now our 16th year. We made it through the abyss. Business was steady and growing; we were up to 40 people; and we were staying current with our bills. We even had enough left over to buy new equipment. I termed out the payables with several of my vendors and paid the balance off over time with interest. Sales kept growing at a steady pace for six years and I was able to clean up the balance sheet. We brought in a new sales manager who knew the product, the market, and the customers, and he began building a strong world-wide network of sales reps. We introduced new products and pursued new markets to broaden our business base. We added CNC machining, expanded our test capability and added a new high-end 3D simulator to expand our design capability. I released a new Windows-CAD package so customers could design filters and see our logo on every printout, and send us the file to have us quote and build the part. After six years of pure hell, we were well on our way to a complete recovery. We bought a building, so we stopped paying rent and with 2.6 acres we could expand when needed. We had seen the light at the end of the tunnel and it was *not* a train.

What This Book Is Not

This is not a how-to book. I am not writing to give you the next whiz-bang marketing strategy, a primer on financial planning, or a human resource guidebook. Though there are discussions and recommendations on how I approach these issues, you'll have to find your own comfort zone.

This book is written more in the vein of *Soup for the Entremanure's Soul* (if there were such a book). I honestly relate incidents, screw-ups, insights and minimally embellished stories of actual events during the first 16 years of the startup and growth of ComNav Engineering. My hope is that some of the lessons I learned will help others avoid the same mistakes I made. But most of all, my message is one of encouragement for all entremanures. (And you know who you are.)

Early days at ComNav

CNC001

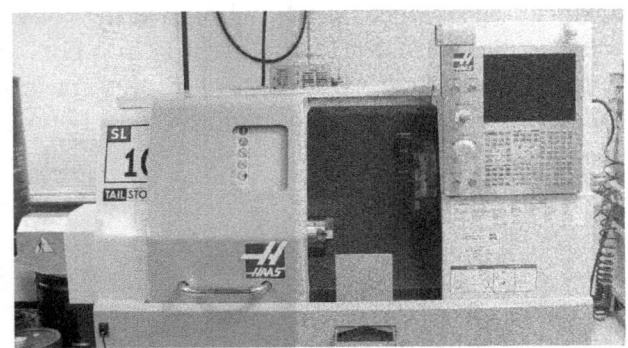

CNC002

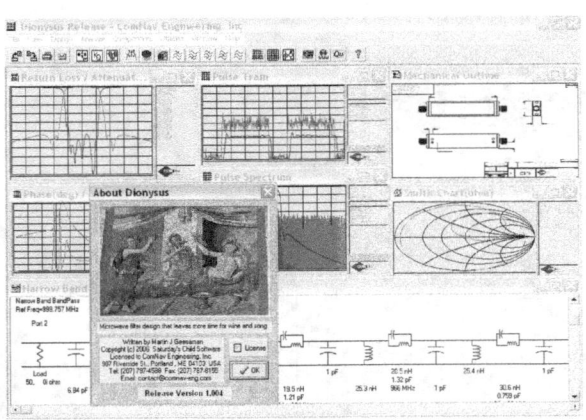

Dionysus

2 Important Principles

Your Family Is Your Lifeboat: Don't Let It Sink

Entremanureship is not a 9 to 5 job. It is all-consuming. When you are not at work, you are thinking about work. But you have to be careful and not let it consume your family. Eventually you will sell or transfer ownership of your company and move on to something else or retire. Your family is with you forever, especially your kids. They need you just as much as your company does and admittedly, it is hard to strike a balance. But you must find a way. The whole point of working in the first place is to support your family. Money alone does not cut it. Speaking from the male perspective, you need to still be the enforcer, the teacher, the guidance counselor, the friend, and above all, Dad to your kids.

Thinking back on it I did not spend as much time with my family as I should have and I regret it. Luckily though by the time ComNav became full-time and we transitioned from a basement operation to a real company, my kids were 11 and 9, so they were both entering the more independent phase of their childhood. I did get to spend a lot of time with them in their early formative years. But when I started putting in long hours in the company, I did miss dinners, helping with their homework and watching TV with them. In the morning I left the house at 7 A.M. and sometimes I didn't get home until 10 P.M., especially during the first year of the company. The only times I saw them was in the morning as we were all getting ready to leave and occasionally when I came home as they were getting ready for bed.

I did, however, keep weekends sacred. Sometimes I went in for a couple of hours in the morning to clean up a job or do some accounting, and the kids sometimes went with me. For the most part I stayed home on the weekends to spend time with my family. I loved doing stuff with my kids (still do!) and we had plenty of memorable moments.

> ### SCAR WARS: Battle #4
>
> One of my favorite memories with my son was the time he started experimenting with model rockets. We walked down the road to a sand pit to set them off. One weekend he had a couple of the biggest engines, but we didn't have a rocket big enough to hold them. So we wondered what would happen if we made a quick and dirty one out of a toilet paper roll.
>
> We took an empty roll and glued on some fins and a straw to ride the launch wire, and glued in the big rocket engine. We brought out the binoculars so we could see it after launch, thinking it would go straight up to non-visible heights.
>
> We set it up in our driveway and did our countdown. We hit the button and WHOOSH! It went up about four feet and then went sideways flying around in a circle about head level. I reacted by jumping on my son and crushing him to the ground where I lay on top of him until the makeshift rocket took off into the woods. Luckily it was after a rain that morning or we could have started a forest fire. I looked up in the window and his mom looked as if she was having an asthma attack, gasping for air from laughing so hard. After we both mooned her, we took off looking for the toilet paper rocket. We never did find it, but no fires started anywhere in our immediate neighborhood so we were very, very lucky.

I also had moments with my daughter. The one that pops up in my mind was at a hockey game. Up to this moment I had always viewed her as my cute little blond princess. I had no concept of the darkness she was capable of.

> **SCAR WARS: Battle #5**
>
> My son's Cub Scout pack had a fundraiser by selling hockey tickets, so we all went to the game. My daughter was about nine at the time and was all about dolls and Beanie Babies. I viewed her as just your average cute, perky, carefree, innocent little girl. It was a hockey game, so of course, a couple of fights broke out. In the second period a fight started right in front of us. All of a sudden my cute little innocent princess of a daughter jumped up on her seat and started screaming, "BLOOD! BLOOD! I WANT TO SEE MORE BLOOD!!!!" I looked up at her with a state of shock on my face and she just shrugged her shoulders and kept on screaming. Ahhh, those special moments of fatherhood.

Though I didn't get to spend as much time with my kids as I wanted, I made sure I was there for their special moments if at all possible. Obviously I couldn't make a recital if I was on a business trip in Europe, but I did my best to avoid conflicts like that. Overall I think I was able to maintain a decent balance, and both my son and daughter are now beginning successful careers. I may not have been Robert Young on *Father Knows Best,* but my kids turned out fine and we have a great relationship. So though I do have some regrets, I was able to start a company without screwing up my kids in the process.

Five Core Principles

There are no hard and fast rules in running a company. Each situation is different and each company has it own eccentricities. But there are some universal concepts that apply across the board. The following list and the subsequent ten items serve as my guideposts when making decisions. They reflect my attitude toward business. I do not make a score card and measure against the list for every decision. But the list is an attempt to refine my decision-making process down to a concise set of ideas I'd like to share.

This all came about when a friend of mine recently bought a small engineering/manufacturing company. The size and scale of his new venture were similar to ComNav Engineering. When we talked on the phone one day, he asked if he could occasionally ask me for advice. I said, "Sure, it's good to have a shoulder to cry on as long as I can use yours, too." One time after we hung up, on a whim I sent him an e-mail containing five principles that I have learned over the last ten years. He liked them so much, he started handing them out, and after I showed them to a couple of my friends, they were also impressed. A couple of people, including my wife, said I should consider writing a book. I really didn't think they were a big deal; I just wrote them out as a whim, and considered them brain droppings. Here are the first five.

Learn from your mistakes and let them go!

Sounds obvious but when someone is dangling a million dollar purchase order under my nose I tap my heels together like Dorothy in the Wizard of Oz and chant *Metricom, Metricom*. A bad decision can be made a lot worse by trying to repair it rather than just chucking it and starting over. Remember the concept of sunk cost. If an investment is bad, leave and move on. The money is gone and isn't coming back; don't let it influence a correct decision for the future.

Get good people and what they need; then stay out of their way.

The quickest way to ruin morale is to constantly second-guess your people, go behind them and micro-manage their work. They have to be competent or you wouldn't have hired them in the first place.

Remember you are the boss.

There is nothing wrong with gathering opinions or a consensus, but always remember it is not a democracy, it is a benevolent dictatorship. It's not your employee's house that's being used as collateral, and they can leave anytime they want. Your signature is on all the documents, so you are the captain and the captain goes down with the ship.

Don't get too bogged down in details.

As a company president your attention span will only be 15 minutes (if you are lucky). I love to program and enjoy working in the lab. But I do not have the luxury of devoting days or even hours to anything. (When I do it takes weeks to recover.) The phone rings; someone needs help; I have to bust up an argument, talk to a vendor and negotiate a contract, yada-yada. But that's okay. Someone has to be the axle the company wheel spins around and that is you.

Your primary job is strategic planning and conflict resolution.

Managing growth is just as important as managing shrinkage. (Think Metricom.) Your primary goal must be long-term sustainable growth. 5%-50% a year is a good range, with the higher growth from multiple customers across multiple market segments. Come up with a plan of where you want to be in incremental years and make decisions that push the company in that direction.

Radical change never works. Even small companies have inertia and will go back to the default position, whatever it was. Make small nudges over time and give them time to take hold and become part of the company's way of doing business.

Conflict resolution is the hardest part of managing your company. There will always be conflict between sales and production, sales and engineering, quality and production, engineering and production, and occasionally the dog will get nervous and piss on the floor. Never take sides; try to nudge the conflict so the players see the solution themselves. Sometimes you will accidentally hire a jerk. Fire him or her quickly before he or she becomes a cancer.

10 More Basic Principles

Your company is your occupation; your family is your life.
Always keep that in perspective. Occasionally I have to be forcefully reminded of that. A frying pan flying across the room at your head does wonders for your memory.

The primary purpose of your company is to make money.
No matter what your product or service, it is only a means to an end. Never forget: The only reason you are in business is to make money.

Treat everyone — employees, vendors, customers, sales reps and even bankers — with honesty and integrity.
Nobody wants to do business with a weasel. Your word is sacred; do not give it unless you mean it and if you give it, follow through. My handshake is more binding than a 10-page contract.

Your employees' productivity reflects how you treat them.
If they feel valued, they will excel; if they are demeaned they will sandbag you

Sales reps are your frontline face to customers.

They must be honest, competent, know your products, and know when to back out and let you take over. If they do not meet these criteria, they can do more harm then good; get rid of them.

Never let a single customer own more than 25% of your capacity.

Losing him can seriously damage your company.

The customer is not always right.

Do not let a customer push you into a bad decision. You aren't the only one at stake; so is the food on your employees' tables.

Never take a loss leader.

You need to make money on every project. It's okay to cut your margin in competitive situations. But if the job is a loser for you, more than likely it will be a loser for your competitors. Be a nice person; let them have it.

Do not do your own payroll.

Find a reputable company and farm it out. I have seen too many people skim payroll taxes and end up in jail. The IRS does not have a sense of humor. Having that much cash sitting in a bank account is way too much temptation when you have a vendor demanding payment. The vendor will be angry at you but he can't put you in jail.

Life is short. Don't take yourself too seriously.

Have fun at work and create a relaxed environment. Not only will you and your employees enjoy coming to work, but also you will actually get more work done.

The title on my business card is not president or CEO. It's Grand Pooh Bah. I use that to convey a sense of whimsy and recognition to business associates and customers. I can't count how many times I have met a customer years after our first meeting and he or she says, "Oh! Grand Pooh Bah!"

The title certainly sticks in people's minds. Even my employees call me *Grand Pooh Bah,* a title I cherish.

Grand Pooh Bah in full regalia

3 The Start-Up

Serendipity

ComNav Engineering's official birthdate is June 1, 1996. I use that date for the company's birthday party, annual stockholders meeting, and anything related to the official start-up date. The significance of that date is that it is the day I signed the lease on our building and we had a real address. Actually the company had been in business in various incarnations since the fall of 1982 as a hobby, and was actually incorporated as a C corporation in Maine in March of 1994 with a dba as Geesaman Software when I began selling Filtroid. Looking back, the critical time that put me on the path to making ComNav Engineering into a real company was the summer of 1992.

It was one of those moments in life where a person comes to a crossroads and recognizes the decision about to be made will have drastic consequences on not only the person, but that person's family as well. Most of the time no one even recognizes those moments looking back, let alone at the time they occur. But this time it was obvious.

I had just been informed that I was going to be laid off from Hughes Aircraft and had begun peppering the country with my resume. After a scary and frustrating few months, I had two job offers, both from ceramic plants. One was at TransTech in Maryland, close to my family, and the company was well established in the RF/Microwave business. The other was at GTE in Maine, 600 miles away, and that company was just in the process of entering the RF/Microwave business. Both opportunities had advantages and disadvantages. The Maryland offer was more money, but I'd be playing second fiddle to an established engineer. The Maine job was far away from home as well. (Did I mention it gets extremely cold <u>in Maine?) I'd</u> be starting up a whole new product line and essentially be working on my own as the only RF/Microwave engineer on staff.

I went back and forth and was driving myself crazy trying to make a decision, until my boss at Hughes gave me what is probably the best advice I had ever received in my life. He told me to stop thinking about it and pick a time, say 7 P.M. Sunday night, and flip a coin. Choose sides. Heads, Maine; tails, Maryland. While the coin is in the air, you will say to yourself, *I hope it's heads!* or *I hope it's tails!* That is your answer. Put the coin in your pocket and never look at it. You just made your decision. That actually worked for me! I packed my family up and moved to Maine.

While I was at Hughes I was taking graduate classes, working toward my Master of Science in Electrical Engineering degree. When I got to Maine the closest school to continue engineering classes was in New Hampshire, 90 minutes away. I still had the urge to continue school so I started taking business classes working toward an MBA. In engineering you have three typical career paths: you can stay technical and go for a PhD, or you can go with an MBA and pursue either management or technical sales. Since my job at GTE was basically a program manager and I would have to sell both to customers and company management, I figured an MBA would yield the most value. Plus I was not into driving three hours a night several times a week. Because of my decision to pursue an MBA, when GTE decided to spin off the filter group, I had the tools and skills to actually pull it off.

On June 1, 1996, I was finishing my last class and had met a friend in school who became my CFO. Both of us graduated together that August and settled in to run and manage ComNav from the beginning with real business knowledge behind us.

While at GTE I was responsible for the technical development of the dielectric resonator line from a RF/microwave perspective. I created all the test procedures, identified potential customers, and did the applications work. After I got that stuff established, I began working on coaxial resonators and filter development. It was around this time I met Lee Perry. He was founder of Perry and Banks advertising and did all the marketing work for this division of GTE. Lee and I hit it off immediately and became fast friends as he developed the marketing materials for the dielectric and coaxial product lines and helped me put together trade show displays. He also helped me come up with the brochures for my software program, Filtroid. At a couple of our creative/drinking meetings I had discussed my dream of starting a filter company and Lee mentioned he was interesting in investing in some kind of manufacturing company. It seemed that at some point down the road we could help each other out.

Along the way I was doing small consulting jobs in my basement and Lee factored my efforts to obtain the needed equipment and raw materials. Basically every time we worked together Lee invested in my efforts and made a decent return on his investment. We had no real timeline for starting a company but figured at some point the timing would be right. How prescient we were still amazes me.

Around the end of 1995 the filter group was beginning to get customers and was becoming a real product line. GTE as a company was starting to get uncomfortable with the coaxial filter product line because it required a completely different business model than what they were used to. It was starting to require more and more resources and the situation was quickly coming to a point where GTE would have to decide whether to go for it or abandon it. Since it required a parallel marketing group and a new set of vendors as well as setting up an external rep network, I was becoming aware that the management was leaning more toward abandonment. The writing was on the wall and I figured my career at GTE was soon to be over. So I wrote up a business plan to make ComNav into a real manufacturing company. At this point

I was thinking of leaving GTE, starting up ComNav from scratch and looking forward to losing money for the first couple of years. It would mean living hand to mouth until I could build a customer base. I showed my plan to Lee and he was interested, but both of us were nervous about jumping off into nothingness. Then word came down that GTE was indeed shutting the filter group down, but would allow me to buy all the equipment for pennies on the dollar. I called Lee to tell him of the decision, and I'll never forget his words, "How much do you need and when do you need it?"

ComNav Engineering, Inc., began operation as a real manufacturing company due to a series of serendipitous events. First was my decision to move to Maine, and getting the opportunity to develop a new product line. In the same timeframe was my getting an MBA and meeting a friend who later became my CFO. And I also met and became friends with Lee, who had the contacts necessary to put the financing together. On top of all that, my biggest customer suddenly decided to go into production, giving us an instant backlog of business. I'd love to say I created ComNav from scratch and fought tooth and nail for survival at the beginning, but it was actually a confluence of unrelated events and I happened to be in the right place at the right time with the right skills.

The fight for survival would happen later.

Initial Financing and Vulture Capitalists

Unfortunately most people do not have a rich relative and have not won the lottery. So other sources are needed for seed money. Depending on the type of business and start up costs, the amount needed can be from a few thousand dollars for a corner bakery to multi-millions for a semiconductor fabrication plant. Although the basic principles still apply, this book is not written for the person starting a semi-fab.

As a rule venture (vulture) capitalists will want a significant ownership percentage. In ComNav's case, my partner, Lee, took 51%, a majority ownership. But we were close friends, had a history together of his factoring some of my previous consulting jobs, and our only partnership agreement was a hand shake. He also put his own house up for collateral. (Talk about trust!) He told me that once the company was up and stable, the company could buy back enough of his stock to make me the majority owner and I trusted him. He never interfered in my decision-making other than the occasional comment, "That was a dumb-ass move." We were always stopping by each other's office for a beer. I kept his brand in-house and he kept mine. I never found out if he would keep his word (though I knew he always would), because he died of a heart attack 18 months after we started the company. I ended up with 85% ownership after the employees put up a 10% down payment and over time the corporation bought back the rest of the shares to buy out most of his estate. Though I was not required to do so, I let his wife hold onto 5% because she asked for it.

Lee and I were the only initial investors in the company. Both of us put our houses on the line and I put some of my GTE severance money in and then lived off the rest, not taking an actual salary from ComNav for the first six months. Lee kept telling me to take a salary, but cash flow was tight and I didn't need a salary at the time. We put together a $350,000 finance package consisting of a $250,000 S.B.A loan and another $100,000 loan from a community development investment group. Since the company was up and running several months before we closed on the loans, Lee kicked in short-term loans so I could meet payroll for my initial staff of four to five people. Later at the closing the bank forced Lee to leave that money in as a long-term loan as part of the overall finance package. So between my investment, Lee's payroll kick-ins, and the two large loans, we started ComNav with $500,000.

I do not consider Lee an actual vulture capitalist, though he did like the title and whenever I called him that he twirled his mustache like some evil cartoon banker. Later when the company got in trouble and we borrowed money from a division of the Finance Authority of Maine, I got my first hardcore experience with a true vulture capitalist. We had vague terms, convertible debentures, misinterpretation of clauses and the state actually trying to take over a percentage of my company. It took three years, but after a failed mediation and my refusing to negotiate and just being a total unreasonable jerk, I won that battle.

Treat Cash Like Water in the Desert

I have seen so many start-ups burn through their initial start-up cash like drunken sailors on leave, I can't even count them all. A prime example was a sales call I made on new customers just starting up and pulled into the parking lot of class A office space. I walked in and they proudly showed off their new mahogany desks, polished brass fixtures, and artwork on the walls. Unless they were sponsored by a vulture capitalist with a massive ego and a bottomless pit of cash and he required this extravagance, this was very rare.

I did not put too much effort in cultivating their business. History has proven they were not going to be around very long. People like this are more interested in the yuppie trappings of business than they are in actually making money. These slicky boys typically do not last out the first year.

The start-ups that have usually turned into the most lucrative longterm business for ComNav, have consisted of a couple of men and their dog in an old strip development, with second-hand furniture, and used equipment purchased at the local HAM fest. A couple years later will come the suits, class A office space and a receptionist who looks like Heather Locklear.

It was about mid-April when the decision was made to shut down the filter line. I wasn't working under a hard deadline to get things up and running, but my customers were. We were still shipping product out of the GTE plant and I was allowed to remain on salary while I was looking around to find a building, make up equipment lists and come up with a start-up timeline for the transition. By the first day of June I had already had two false starts on locations, and had ordered most of the equipment from school lab equipment, office supply, and tool supply companies. I needed a place to have all this stuff delivered.

Around this time I went into GTE for a meeting with the CFO to work out the last minute details of the equipment I needed and what they were going to charge me for it. In the process of our conversation, I was telling him of all the equipment I had ordered and he congratulated me on getting the financing already. I told him the truth and said it hadn't come in yet and the banks were dragging their feet. He inquired how I was getting all the equipment delivered. I said, "There are these wonderful things called purchase orders, where you fill them out with what you want, send them to people, and they send you stuff."

Being an accountant, he failed to see the humor of my comments. But we continued on and he finally said, "Hey, that's your problem not mine. As long as we eventually get paid for this equipment, that's all I care about." Around GTE I had a reputation for being a bull in a china shop, but I was an honest bull.

I stayed up late <u>in the night at </u>my home office which served as the temporary company headquarters. My desk was covered with equipment catalogs as I made shopping lists. Once I had it all figured out, I needed to buy about $200,000 worth of tools, lab and office equipment, reflow ovens, and computers. This did not include the over $80,000 I needed to pay GTE for the equipment I was taking with me. So now that I had the list, I just needed to figure out from where I was going to get it. I used Lee's company as a credit reference and started sending out purchase orders.

To give you an insight into my relationship with Lee, he called up and asked to see the list of equipment I was buying. I faxed it to him. He called me back thirty minutes later and asked, "Why the hell are you buying a full size plastic doctor's office skeleton?"

I responded, "Because I don't have one."

He said, "Oh, okay."

Between the two of us, that was actually considered a rational conversation. Actually the skeleton was the only extravagant thing I bought, and it has brought us an infinite amount of entertainment for years in the form of practical jokes, silly ceremonies, and general all-around stupidity. Lee even borrowed it for his office at one point.

As I mentioned previously I didn't take a salary for the first six months while the company was getting up and running. By that time we were receiving payments from customers for shipped product and actually had positive cash flow. But in the meantime I did have to pay my employees. At that point I had a Draftsman/IT person, a CFO, an engineer, an assembler and a tech, for a total payroll of about $3,000 a week.

Obviously it takes time to get raw materials, build and test the parts, and then wait the 30+ days to get paid by the customer. Plus there were turn-on costs for utilities, and the initial first and last months' rent for our space and riggers to move the heavy equipment. All this was up and running and our financing still had <u>not come through</u>. I was at Lee's office pretty much every Friday with a six of his favorite brew, saying "Lee, Ol' buddy, Ol' pal...." He came through every week and got us through until the bankers got us through underwriting.

At times it did get pretty hairy and caused some friction with his partner, but he hung in there and stood by us.

Wearing Many Hats

Designer, Materials Manager, Shipper, Assembler, Technician, Quality, Janitor, or whatever functions your specific business requires—all these are titles you can apply to yourself in the startup phase. These functions have to be done and the only people around to delegate to are facing you in the mirror. You may like to call yourself president or CEO, but if the toilet clogs up, you will be the one grabbing the plunger. Typically in a manufacturing company there are at least a few people with you and you end up swapping tasks back and forth. Whoever sees something that needs to be done, does it. Whoever answers the phone does the follow up. Whoever is in the office when the cold-call salesman walks in, kicks him out. If you are the kind of person who sees him/herself in a suit, ordering people around, then go get a corporate job. Starting a company requires getting your hands dirty. But if having your own company is your dream, it can be a labor of love.

Initially there were less than a dozen of us. We each had our specific job functions, but everyone chipped in on everything. If the drafter didn't have anything to draft, then he was out washing or labeling filters. The engineer not only designed and prototyped the product, but also ran a surface grinder, assembled parts and tuned and shipped them. The CFO was out on the production floor pitching in where extra hands were needed. I was on the phone talking to customers, hiring new reps and also out on the floor to help build and tune product. And then I'd make the 7:15 P.M. rush to FedEx to ship to the customer. It sounds like it was a madhouse and it was, but we had a blast. We were creating something new; we had the freedom and flexibility to fit in and do what felt right and was needed; and every day was a new challenge. Did we screw up? Oh yeah! We made some really boneheaded mistakes, but we worked together, solved the problems and continued on.

SCAR WARS: Battle #6

When everyone was on a learning curve and there were incidents galore. Every day we came to work and laughed our butts off.

We had Exacto knife fights. (No one was hurt.)

One of our guys came to work wearing a long black trench coat one day about the time of the Columbine massacre. He also brought an electrical cartridge fuse.

Someone else thought it was a bomb, grabbed it and threw it into the woods behind our building.

4 The Market
Be Careful in Defining Your Market

Marketing is to selling as strategy is to tactics. In defining your market you are defining your company to the world. Your market defines your product base, your potential customers, your sales territory and your overall brand. There are potential problems when defining your market. You can make your definition too narrow and limit your potential customers, or you can define it too broadly and minimize your brand by trying to be everything to everyone and your sales force will lose focus.

A classic example of defining your market too narrowly is the railroad industry at the turn of the last century. They saw themselves as being in the railroad business rather than the transportation business. Then with the development of long-haul trucking, they did not see themselves as competing with trucks and lost a significant amount of business as well as initially missed the opportunity to invest in trucking. Eventually they saw the light and multimode transportation systems developed, combining rail and truck freight lines.

They were also able to minimize the damage from later loss of passenger traffic to the airlines. The railroads were able to survive but they missed an opportunity to vastly expand their business at the outset. Now most multimode transportation companies consist of both rail and truck operations or partnerships between the two.

An example of the consequences of defining your market too broadly would be Sears Roebuck. At one point they were the world's largest retailer and everyone got the Sears catalog in the mail. They were the standard that all retail operations were measured against. Then they expanded into automotive repair, credit cards, financial services, real estate, car rentals, yada, yada <u>and lost their focus</u>. Walmart came on the scene and Sears was caught with their pants down. By focusing solely on retail and creating an extremely efficient nationwide distribution system, Walmart cleaned Sears' clock by creating efficiencies of scale and could drastically undercut Sears on pricing. As a result Sears has been on the precipice of bankruptcy for the last couple of years and has very little chance of reclaiming its past glory.

In my industry defining your market too broadly has even worse consequences. Not only do you lose your niche, but also it actually becomes exponentialy more difficult and expensive to sell. The microwave component business for the most part is based on manufacturers' representatives' ability to find new opportunities and get design wins. The industry is very diversified with each company generally specializing in a single component. Reps typically have a line card of a dozen or more companies they represent and are unwilling to give up profitable lines if you decide to expand your product line into other areas that conflict with their existing principles.

Reps have to eat, too, and if you come up with a new product line that is a conflict with an existing profitable line, there is a good chance you will be dropped. It doesn't matter what great drinking buddies you are: Business comes first. If they already have a principle that is profitable on that line, they are not going to be willing to do the missionary work to help get you established in this new area. They have already done that once, so why do it again? In addition to the problems with sales, your engineering staff will also become overworked and lose focus and there is a good chance your internal sales staff will limit themselves to picking low-hanging fruit and forego the potentially big jobs that have a lot of front-end engineering overhead on them.

In my situation we make high volume custom filters. In addition to component types we limit our sales efforts to take on projects that will ultimately result in long-term sustainable business. Even in our narrow product line of filters we do not try to be everything to everybody. There are three of us in the company who can design and I view it as a wasted effort to go after small quantity short-run jobs that will only yield a few thousand dollars in sales. The opportunity cost of small jobs with limited returns is just not worth it when compared to investing engineering time into a job that can run for years and generate hundreds of thousands of dollars.

This is a company efficiency issue more than a sales issue. It becomes more of a sales issue if we start going after mixers, couplers, amplifiers and other components that could generate a conflict with several of our reps. In that case the result would be that I would have to either get established with new reps (which takes a long time), or create my own international sales staff, an extremely expensive prospect.

In the first couple of years of ComNav I made the mistake of defining my market too narrowly. I decided to stick primarily in the high volume commercial market. Concentrating on ceramic filters and forgoing most LC and cavity type filters, I was going to be the premier ceramic filter supplier and leave the other stuff to my competitors. We did do some limited LC and cavity filters but it was difficult for us to compete since we had limited machining capability and farmed most of that out to local vendors. That was both expensive and time consuming. At the time in the mid-1990s this seemed to be where most of the business in my niche was. The military applications had yet to fully accept the ceramic filters we specialized in since they were new to the market and had little long-term reliability history.

As we approached the year 2000, we started to move toward the military business and started to slowly expand in LC and cavity filters, but I was not pursuing it due to all the additional documentation and overhead required. This was a major mistake that almost killed my company. When the tech bubble burst, most of my major customers went bankrupt, some not even pausing at Chapter 11 but going straight to Chapter 7. As I mentioned previously we went from 80 people down to six and from $1.5M per month in sales down to $60K per month. It was a terrible time and we almost didn't make it. I started quoting on anything that came along just to keep the lights on.

By this time military companies had come to embrace ceramic technology and we were being forced by circumstances to go after more and more military jobs despite my hesitation. However this turned out to be a good thing because military projects are longterm and last for years. Once you are designed in, you can pretty much bank on that business coming back around every other quarter or so. They basically become annuities and they go a long way in leveling out the extreme ups and downs of the commercial business. So now I try to maintain a balance of as close to 50/50 military/commercial as I can to keep the production flow leveled out and maintain a steady and reasonable growth rate.

Expanding the Niche

It's really hard to break into the military market. It took us two years to get into Raytheon. After we got them under our belts, Scott Pusey, Vice President of Sales and Marketing, targeted other military accounts. The reason military accounts are so difficult to break into is that they are leery of trying new vendors. In addition they are especially particular about quality and performance, requiring additional documentation and testing.

Initially we started doing only commercial work and had no military contracts. We wouldn't even consider government work because the quality requirements and extra paperwork required would have been too much for our resources at the time. Now we take it on and subcontract the environmental work. We have a balance between commercial and military. Usually when one is strong the other is weak, and vice versa. In the middle of the market are industrial applications.

The big advantage with military contracts is that programs to which they are attached can last years or even decades. So the business is like an annuity and provides a steady stream of work where the orders just show up. Once you have print position on a military spec, it is very difficult for your competitors to come in behind you and grab the business from you.

During the commercial boom of the late '90s, some of our competitors switched from military to commercial contracts and left the military high and dry. After the bust they had difficulty getting back into the military business and that gave us a window of opportunity. Since we were new to the market and didn't have a reputation yet, the switch was fortuitous for us and we picked up some good military contracts.

"How would a businessman know it's time to make this switch? How do you identify a pivotal moment in your company's history? In our case it was hiring Scott and his background. He had the experience, skills and contacts to assist us in breaking into this part of the market. But he had to drag me kicking and screaming. I would much rather make a thousand $20 parts than ten $2,000 parts with a book of documentation for each one. But as opportunities arose we looked at each one and made the decision to go ahead if it fit our business model, so we made the transition gradually. It wasn't a quick, huge switchover; we slowly upped our percentage of military work while still doing commercial work. As we expanded we went after more and more military work. Then there is space-qualified work which is exponentially more difficult than military work. We're not considering it yet, but we may at some point.

Find a Market Niche with Minimal Competition

To generate customer loyalty, build some exclusivity into your product line. If you can provide a product that is difficult for your competitors to produce, you don't have to worry about them trying to second-source you and cut into your business. Whether it is microwave filters, coffee, stereo sales, or pretty much any product or service, you can find an underserved niche. This can be a segment that is either too hard, too easy, too low a margin, in no-man's land between big and small companies, or another unique characteristic.

In my industry filter companies typically fall into one of two categories. On one extreme are the highly specialized, very high-volume filter companies, making a minimal number of specific products and service-specific applications. The Japanese are very good at this and they dominate this end of the market. On the other extreme are the companies with a very broad product-line making every type of filter imaginable, but not so good at high volume. Most of the US and European companies dominate this end of the market. ComNav's niche is in the middle with custom high-volume projects. The big companies do not want to do custom work; they design their products for specific applications like GPS and cell phones, and make millions of these products each year.

Most custom specialty houses have such a broad product line they have not taken the time to develop the custom production fixturing and processes required for consistent, large-volume, quality production. Most of their products are made one at a time and they concentrate on making each part work rather than on production yield. Due to this different mindset they tend to have a hard time competing and shy away from high volume. Coming from a product line spinoff of a large automotive manufacturer, we had it beaten into our heads that we need to design for high volume. As a result of this intense training, when a new product comes along we design the production process as well as the product. Due to our custom manufacturing techniques, most of the time our competitors can't duplicate one of our parts, let alone thousands.

Create and Protect Your Brand

Ideally when talking to potential customers they will already have a positive notion about your company. This only happens if you have been successful in creating a positive brand for your company and products.

Your brand doesn't just concern your product, it concerns all aspects of your company. Yes it is reflective of the performance and quality of your product, but it also encompasses the customer's total experience of working with your company. Are employees pleasant when talking on the phone? Are questions and issues taken care of in a timely manner? How quickly are problems resolved? Does the customer get the feeling that he or she is important? Is it actually a pleasant experience to work with your company?

In addition to having a good product reputation, we go out of our way to come across as being a fun company to do business with. Our sales assistant is always bubbly and happy on the phone even when she is having a bad day. People like her are a rare find, but they do exist and she is the perfect person to be on the front lines of customer contact. In addition there are several lighthearted techniques we use to keep things amusing. For example at trade shows we have given out whoopee cushions with our company logo screen-printed on them. On our voice mail system you can select option six to discuss migrating coconuts. Most employees who have contact with the outside world have humorous messages on their phones' voice mail. This type of behavior is not only tolerated, it is strongly encouraged. The net effect of this is to present an image of ComNav as a fun company to do business with, and it is all about the company brand.

ComNav Engineering is known for complex designs and high quality products. Advertising is one way to project a brand, but industry gossip is infinitely more powerful, both good and bad. Word travels very quickly in any industry through reps, salesmen, vendors, staff moving around to different companies, and general industry gossip. If you get a bad reputation as a schlock house, it is almost impossible to overcome. There is an old saying that one complaint does more damage than the praise of ten atta-boys can fix. This is especially true because a lot of customers don't complain; they just don't come back. In this case you have potentially lost a customer and don't even know how or why. I am very protective of ComNav's brand and will go to pretty much any extreme to protect our reputation. If we screw up a job, I will do what it takes to try and make it up to that customer.

One example of how far I'll go to protect my brand is a cavity job we did years ago. It was one of the first times we ventured into Puck/Cavity filters, which are basically made of ceramic donuts mounted on plastic pedestals. I screwed up the design and the pedestals kept snapping off. The customer called and I gave him our FedEx number to ship a part back. I popped the lid and immediately realized I had created a major design flaw. The customer was on the opposite side of the country and production was shut down; the situation could not have been worse. It was Wednesday morning and by the following Monday I had redesigned the pedestal, found a rush machine shop, got new pedestals made, and flew out two of my techs with a network analyzer and a box of new pedestals. We had all the parts fixed in less than a week and the customer was shut down for only three days. The customer was so impressed with how far I would go to back my product, we got an order for another 1000 parts two weeks later. In the long run by taking drastic action, I made ten times more money than I would have by not backing the product, not to mention potential legal liability (though I didn't even think of the possible legal consequences until it was all over).

Occasionally you will run into a situation that no matter what you do, the customer will not be satisfied. All people are different and it happens. Don't let it get you down or reflect on your dealings with other customers. It's just a fact that you can't please all the people all the time. If people are turned off by the way we do business I have generally found it would have eventually turned into a sour relationship anyway.

After over 16 years of doing business this way, most of our customers are long-term relationships and are considered more friends than just customers. It has come to the point where we win business on our reputation alone before I even provide a quote to a customer. An engineer whom we have worked with in the past will change jobs and it is not uncommon for us to soon become his new company's primary filter source, even though we have never done business with them in the past. This occurs primarily due to our past relationship with their new engineer.

Market Your Products as Broadly as Possible

As the name implies, ComNav Engineering is an electronics engineering and manufacturing company. We manufacture custom microwave filters. As far as electronic components go, we are pretty far down the food chain when a new system is designed. Since almost every transmitter-receiver system needs filters, our products can cover a wide range of applications from simple communication systems to WiFi, to GPS to military command and control systems. When we first started we primarily concentrated on wireless networking, and various commercial communications applications. This worked well for the first year or so. The problem is that the electronics industry is extremely volatile. Sales forecasts are more the work of Ouija boards than logical analysis. So business goes up and down seemingly at random. But it is also very diverse. There are communications, GPS navigation, medical, public service, military, satellite communication, IFF, and on and on. Typically when the commercial market is up, the military market is down and vice versa. The goal is to sell into as many applications as possible to smooth out the fluctuations in business.

The breadth of applications that we have been designed

into actually can boggle the mind. We are designed into sheep tags in New Zealand, GPS receivers in smart artillery shells, the EZPass system that covers the East Coast's toll roads and bridges, tractors in the Midwest to minimize fuel use with accurate plowing, the US Congress for a WiFi system, in building communications in the Petronas Twin Towers in Malaysia and the list goes on and on. The nice thing about filters is that as a component it is so far down the food chain, the total list of potential applications is well beyond imagination. From sheep tags to smart artillery... well you get the idea.

Finding these applications is the job of the sales reps. It doesn't matter if it is the local rep covering your home territory or your rep covering the Pacific Rim or Eastern Europe, a good rep knows every company in his or her territory and has working relationships with the design engineers. When a new application comes up, the rep either gets a call from the engineers or discovers it on a visit by asking the engineers if there is anything new on the horizon. If the design is relatively straightforward, most of the front end initial simulation and quote work can be done via email or phone with the rep providing translation services if necessary. If the project is on the bleeding edge and requires trade-offs between different components, a visit from a plant engineer may be required to establish the relationship and build confidence in the customer by working closely together. This is especially the case if this is a new customer that you haven't worked with before and you are an unknown quantity. It is all part of creating the initial perception of you, your product and your company to start building that perception of your brand you are trying to create in your customers' minds.

Your Competitors Are Not Your Enemies

You are trying to make a buck, your competitors are trying to make a buck, and occasionally you are both going after the same buck. Your competitors keep you focused and force you not to sit back and take it easy. Know your competitors. Which niche do they excel in? What are their capabilities? Do they have a tendency to use predatory sales techniques? Do not trash your competitors to the customer; in the end it makes you look like a weasel. It is okay to point our differences, your advantages, and performance differences. Don't disparage your competitors because most of the time they will do that function well enough on their own.

We have one competitor who is constantly trying to come in behind us and steal our business. Even to the point of losing money on a job just to knock us out. I don't know what I did to get on his dark side but this appears to have been an ongoing priority for him for many years now. The funny thing is that it usually ends up blowing up in his face and we get a big laugh out of it once all the details are known. The following represents just two examples where I know all the details, though there have been other instances also.

The first time I was aware it had happened, we were both going after a filter job at an East Coast Communications Company. The application was a legacy product that was nearing the end of its product life cycle. Both of us had supplied tens of thousands of this part over the years. The customer wanted pricing for an annual blanket order of 20,000 parts but only wanted to place orders quarterly for 5,000 parts with no hard commitment for the balance. I had already been burned by one of these deals before and wasn't willing to stick my neck out without the full commitment. In order to give the customer the price he wanted, I needed to buy all the raw material at once and then store it. They were custom parts that could only be used for this product, so I told the customer to either give me the full order or pay the 5000-piece price, a difference of about 20%. The customer tried to play me off against my competitor and said he wanted to give the order to me because my parts were slightly better on one of the specs, but my competitor was willing to meet his terms. I wished him luck and told him to give it to my competitor. The only order placed was for the first 5,000 parts and then the project died.

The second time it happened was with a customer we were doing serious production for, about 50,000 parts per year. My competitor wanted in but could not meet the production volume with consistent specs. The customer was constantly beating us up on price but since we were the only ones who could meet both the spec and the volume, their options were limited. Then eventually our competitor found a supplier in Japan that could produce a part with close enough specs out of a single block of ceramic. The customer accepted it so they could have a second source and gain some leverage on us. Our competitor bought a bunch of these parts and tooled up a carrier board to match our part and offered it to the customer at a significant discount. At the time the customer was in a redesign mode and was not ordering any product.

They anticipated another big run and I believe they ordered a few thousand parts from our competitor who was actually shipping at a loss due to their large yield hits of parts that did not meet the specs. I later learned form our rep that the big production run never happened and manufacturing of that system was shut down. So my competitor spent all kinds of money in tooling and parts and lost money in the process and was left holding a large amount of custom inventory that could go nowhere, all in an effort to knock us out. My rep later told me that we made all the money there was to be made on that project. The competitor's part never did perform as well as ours and he never got a large order for it.

Do I hold any animosity toward this man? No, not really. I do find it kind of entertaining that he is always nipping at my heels like an angry Yorkie. But it does keep me on my toes and makes me realize that if I start taking things for granted, there is always somebody right there to replace me. I firmly believe that healthy competition makes both parties stronger, and gives the customers the best solution to their technical problems. If we start just phoning in designs and stop trying to make the best part possible, there will always be someone there who makes that extra effort and we will lose the job. So I do not mind competition as long as it's fair and there is no behind-the-scenes activity going on to tilt the playing field. So far I have not seen that as an issue.

> **SCAR WARS: Battle #7**
>
> We knew we needed a quality control manual. Our quality manager at the time bought a manual online and edited it to suit our business.
>
> She had taken a boat-building manual and cut and pasted stuff, but she missed some of the boat material.
>
> When the inspector came, he asked me to see the keel room.
>
> What keel room?

5 Selling Your Products

Sales Reps Exponentially Increase Your Presence

In ComNav Engineering's industry, products are typically sold through commissioned sales representatives. It is an inexpensive way to create a worldwide sales force and you only pay them when they sell. Typically a sales rep has a line card with a dozen or so principles. So in addition to our filters they will also be selling mixers, amplifiers, semiconductors, couplers, connectors, pretty much everything a system design engineer needs.

The best sales reps in my industry are ex-engineers. Make sure your reps know your capabilities, product line, and the market niche you are looking for. Your goal for your sales reps is the Design Win: to have your product designed into the customers' systems. Since there is no industry standard packaging, once you are designed in, your competitors have to play catch up. Since you are looking for design wins, structure your commission plan to compensate that activity. ComNav only pays commission on design wins.

If the end product is manufactured in another territory, the design-win rep gets all the commission, causing a problem with some reps initially who are used to getting commission on anything sold in their territory. Once the product is designed and being built by a board-stuffer, the board-stuffer rep adds no value to the transaction. So why should he be allowed to milk the commission?

It typically takes three years for a project to go from initial concept to production. There is a lot of back and forth and the design-win rep must put in a lot of time and effort in missionary work. He needs to know and have confidence that his effort will be rewarded when the project matures.

Trade Shows Generally Are Not Worth the Money

There are two conditions when I think trade shows are worth the time and money to have a display booth. The first is when you are just starting out and you need to establish at least a minimal market presence. At that point no one knows who you are so a trade show is a great place for your coming-out party. Don't expect to make any sales though. In the almost 30 years that I have been attending trade shows, I have booked one order. We didn't even have a booth! We were just walking the show and our rep introduced us to a customer we had already been talking to and the customer handed us a purchase order. Generally speaking, trade shows are more about marketing than selling.

The second condition when trade shows are important is if you are protecting your position as market leader. In that case you need to go all out, rent multiple spaces and have a large presence.

We did our main industry trade show for the first five years of the company's existence. In typical ComNav fashion we did it with a sense of whimsy. We refused to wear suits like everyone else and wore khakis and custom polo shirts. A couple years after we first did it, khakis and polo shirts became standard trade show attire. In addition to changing the fashion we also gave away whimsical swag. Almost everyone gave away candy, pens, note pads, various calculators and other useful things. We gave away custom printed whoopee cushions, imprinted yoyos, beer huggies, design software and various unusual items through the years. My attitude was this: The stranger the giveaway, the more people would remember you.

The year we gave away whoopee cushions I had one of my pet theories confirmed. An elderly Chinese woman approached our booth carrying an armload of brochures and giveaways. She had a PhD in engineering and was attending the seminars. She stopped and asked what our whoopee cushion was. Since she could barely speak English, we couldn't quite get it across, so I decided a demonstration was in order.

My partner distracted her and I blew one of the cushions up nd put it on the chair. Then I asked her if she would like to sit and rest a minute. She obliged and the whoopee cushion worked excellently, nice and loud. The look of embarrassment and confusion on her face was priceless as she jumped up from the chair, her armful of brochures flying everywhere. Turning around she saw the whoopee cushion and said, "Ooooh...*whoopee cushion!*" and then laughed so hard tears came to her eyes. This proves my pet theory that no matter your age, gender, nationality or level of education: Farts are funny.

Limit Customer's Access to Your Capacity

One of the biggest lessons I've learned is never allow one customer to exceed 25% of your business unless it is done on your terms with longterm contracts with non-cancellable, non-pushout clauses and with prepayments, and/or cancellation fees. If the customer balks, then he isn't confident enough in his own business plan to partner with you and chances are you will be left holding the bag and forced to layoff a significant portion of your staff. This is the classic putting-all-your-eggs-in-one-basket scenario. Allowing a single customer to consume more than 25% of your capacity will make your company susceptible to every hiccup and cough of that customer. Even if you have to share the business with a competitor on a license basis or walk away, don't do it. Trust me, you do not want to stand in front of a room of 30 or more people who put their financial future in your hands and tell them they no longer have a job. Your primary goal over and above everything is the long-term health of your company, not short-term growth.

Make Statements with Your Advertising

Advertising can be used for more than just selling your product. You can use it to display your company culture, comment on industry issues, deal with customer complaints and most fun of all, insult your competition. I was on a sales trip once and on three different customer visits, the customers were complaining that one of my competitors told them that they lost the recipe and would not supply a part the customer had previously purchased. I had been in this business long enough to know that they did not lose the recipe. Either the engineer who did it left and his work was not documented well enough, or more than likely, they lost money on the job and either they were too scared to go back to the customer with the true price or the customer refused to pay it. When I got home, my partner, Lee, came over to drink a few beers and asked how the trip went and I told him about losing the recipe. After a few Coors for me and a couple Rolling Rocks for him, we came up with the *Chef Marty never loses his recipes* ad shown on the next page. We ran it in a couple of trade magazines and it was actually our first ad. I found out a few months later at a trade show that it was a direct hit.

During a sales meeting at my competitor's place of business, the sales manager discussed our ad by slamming his fist on the table and saying, "...and #*?!# Marty..." Score!!

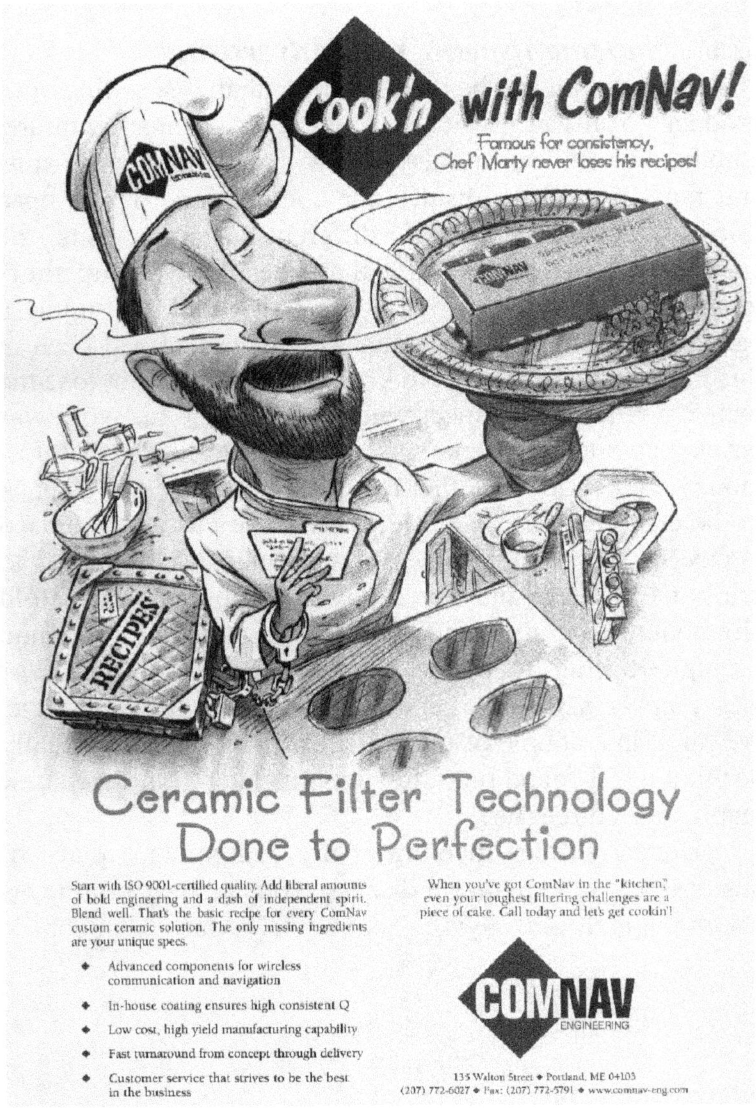

Cook'n with ComNav!

Famous for consistency, Chef Marty never loses his recipes!

Ceramic Filter Technology
Done to Perfection

Start with ISO 9001-certified quality. Add liberal amounts of bold engineering and a dash of independent spirit. Blend well. That's the basic recipe for every ComNav custom ceramic solution. The only missing ingredients are your unique specs.

- Advanced components for wireless communication and navigation
- In-house coating ensures high consistent Q
- Low cost, high yield manufacturing capability
- Fast turnaround from concept through delivery
- Customer service that strives to be the best in the business

When you've got ComNav in the "kitchen," even your toughest filtering challenges are a piece of cake. Call today and let's get cookin'!

135 Walton Street ◆ Portland, ME 04103
(207) 772-6027 ◆ Fax: (207) 772-5791 ◆ www.comnav-eng.com

Always Do Business on Your Terms, Not Your Customer's

It is pretty much Darwinian how big companies try to bully little companies. I cannot tell you how many times I have heard customers, especially board-stuffers, say, "That's how we do business; that's our policy." My response is always, "Well, it's not my policy and if you want my parts, these are the terms. Big companies think they are doing you a favor by doing business with you. It is not a favor if they give you a million-dollar purchase order, you buy the materials, hire staff, set up a production line, and then they cancel two months into the project.

Ask the man you just were forced to lay off how appreciative he is of the favor your customer bestowed upon him. Come up with terms that work for your business and enforce them across the board to every customer from the two men and their dog in a garage to Motorola and AT&T. Never, never, sign a customer's order acknowledgement. If you do it means you agree to their terms instead of yours.

Work with Your Customers, Not for Them

Since we make custom products and every design is at least slightly different, we form close relations with the design engineers with whom we initially work. Once a design is mature and the product is in production, invariably the accountants get involved and filters are generally the most expensive part of the system. At that point we are generally under pressure to reduce costs. We already have a sliding price scale based on quantity, since like most products, you can get decent economies of scale on larger quantities. The raw materials are cheaper; the fixed costs are spread over more parts; yields typically go up as the design is optimized through successive production lots, and your people get faster and more efficient as experience sets in. usually this automatic price reduction keeps the accountants happy.

Occasionally a customer has an aggresive pricing strategy. It could be a competitive product and one of your competitors is nipping at your heels. The volume has become so big it justifies developing a high volume popcorn part, which are expensive to develop on the front end but are made by the millions for a few dollars each. At this point you have to decide how much you want to keep the business, how low you are willing to cut your margin, and if you can still make money.

It is extremely important to know your actual costs and your production capacity. Two factors come into play: *How much capacity am I selling to the customer?* And *What's the cash flow on that capacity?* If it gets to the point where you are generating 25% of your cashflow by using 50% of your capacity, it is time to walk away or share the production. Every product has a product life cycle where you can make money. In our case, especially in the commercial world, we will ride a job through proto-typing, pre-production and the first few years of production and then serious cost-cutting begins and specs are sacrificed in favor of costs and the part goes to a high-volume popcorn part. At that point we have made all the money we could on that project, and it's time to start looking for the next job. Incidentally you really should always be looking for that next job.

> **SCAR WARS: Battle #8**
> Kirk has a tendency to be accident prone. When he didn't know how to remove the grinding wheel, he took a bar and put it in the Y and it slipped off, lacerating his finger on the chuck. Blood everywhere. He needed stitches and had to wear a big metal thing on his pinkie. Another culprit is a Drummel tool with a diamond on the end. We've all been drilled by the diamond and all who tune filters have nicks on their fingers and thighs from that tool!

6   The Product
What We Do

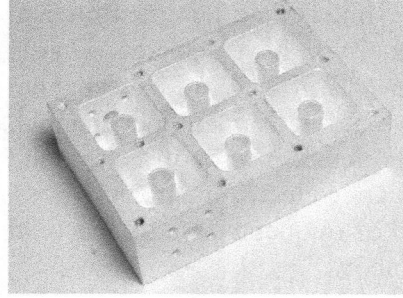

Our business card explains the meaning of our company's name: ComNav. We make custom engineered parts for wireless communication and navigation systems.

Actually the name came from my days in the Navy when I was stationed with an A6E Intruder squadron at the state of Washington's Whidbey Island. I was an aviation Electronics Technician assigned to the ComNav shop (*Com* for communications and *Nav* for navigation). The name sounded cool so I appropriated it.

The core business of ComNav Engineering is microwave filters. Our primary, core technology is ceramic filters. Over the years we have expanded into discreet inductor/capacitor filters, and cavity filters, but we are known in the industry as primarily a ceramic filter company. For non-engineers, I'll explain what a filter is <u>without being</u> too geeky.

Filters separate out different frequency bands of electro-magnetic waves. Any time you have a receiver/transmitter combination, you need a method to make the receiver sensitive in its working band, and make sure a transmitter only transmits in its working band. As an example, a TV set receives all the channels at the same time. The reason you can select and watch only one is that there is a filter in there that filters out the channel you have selected. That is why you can watch *Two and a Half Men* on one channel without *Oprah* bleeding in on top of it from another channel. Another analogy would be to picture a rainbow. Light and colors are just very high frequency electro-magnetic waves. Each color is a different band of frequencies; a filter would select one color out of the rainbow.

We have built our initial reputation on passive microwave filters using mature technology we already possessed and exploiting new technologies as they become available. Typical products consist of various kinds of filters and filter subsystems constructed of lumped, distributed, ceramic, and hybrid technologies. The focus of our primary marketing effort consists of high volume, custom parts for wireless applications in the DC to 20 GHz frequency range, for commercial, military and space applications. By exploiting new technologies such as ceramic resonators and surface mount packaging, ComNav Engineering has become an industry innovator instead of falling into the me-too role of many of the current industry players.

I have always pushed the fact that customer service will always be the major cornerstone of ComNav's operations. A common complaint I've heard on many sales trips is the lack of timely response to requests and the general lack of keeping the customer informed of job progress. I make a point that ComNav Engineering places a strong emphasis on customer relations and solving complex engineering problems.

Though the company actually manufactures microwave filters, the company's <u>true product is</u> engineering expertise.

The natural give and take that occurs during the design process allows us to form a close relationship with our customers. With engineering talent and modern design software, ComNav Engineering is in an excellent position to provide a quick response to customer needs and solve complex engineering problems.

Competitive and Non-competitive Products

Most companies start because they are based on some kind of innovation: a new way of doing something, a new manufacturing technique, or a new business philosophy distinguishing them from the competition. When we were in the research and design phase at GTE, we had three years to develop products and processes without having to meet customer deadlines. We could take our time, finding out what worked and what didn't. As a result we developed a few innovative design techniques that are unique to us. This gives us an advantage over our competition by allowing us to produce parts in large volume with performance that few of our competitors can do in prototpye quantities. When we are in our niche of high volume/high performance, we can get a higher margin on our products. When we face competition obviously we have to price with lower margins to win the business. This is still good business as long as we are making some profit and it keeps production running.

The Five Fickle Fingers of Fate

A common joke among myself and a few friends who also have companies are the five fickle fingers of business fate: "Price, Performance, Service, Quality, Delivery: pick two." It sounds like a cop-out, but no matter how hard you try, it is almost impossible to have all five in any given product. So you have to set your priorities based on what is most important to both you and your customer. At ComNav I try to prioritize quality above all else. Bad quality can do more damage to your company than anything else. It can cost you money in wasted time and materials and can severely damage your reputation with your customers. How you recover from a mistake is just as important as the initial quality of the product.

This leads to the next priority: service. Customers like to be coddled and kept in the loop. A good customer relationship will go a long way in dealing with other issues in a calm rational manner if they blow up in your face. The next priority is delivery. The last thing you want to do is shut down a customer's production line. It is almost impossible to recover the relationship if you shut them down. Performance is usually a given with us. Most of the time customers come to us because they need something special and custom. Finally comes price. Believe it or not most of the time price is not an issue with our end-customers as long as it's reasonable. When it goes into production at a board-stuffer, they will try to squeeze every penny out of you but most of our product is custom. We are on the bill of materials. So they have to just suck it up.

Know Where the Edge of the Cliff Is

For us every product is a new design and a mini R&D project. Since we are designing new products, at times we do not know where the limit of the technology is and we occasionally cross it. The hardest thing for me to learn initially was to say no to a customer. I tried to be everything to everybody and occasionally ended up with a smelly turd in the engineering lab that lost us significant money. Know where your limits are and what it takes to make money on a job. Then don't let the customer push you over that line. At ComNav we like to push the edge because it allows us to produce products that our competitors can't match, and minimizes competition. But occasionally we design ourselves off a cliff. Then customer relations are critical. Usually the customer knows you are pushing the edge because nobody else was stupid enough to quote the job in the first place. 99% percent of the time you can work out a compromise solution with the customer. It is that remaining 1% that is totally ego-crushing and is hard to forget. But at some point you have to face the customer and admit that you screwed up. At that point your best scenario is to salvage the relationship for hope of future business.

Patents are Scratchier than Toilet Paper

And they are not worth as much. Each industry is, of course, different. In the electronic components industry a patent does nothing but make lawyers rich and offer less than zero protection to your inventions. In fact since you have to fully describe your invention in a patent application, you may as well buy an ad and show the world how to build your products. The problem lies in the patent law itself. You can patent devices but not technologies. Because of this all a competitor has to do is look up your patent, change one component and it is a new device. Companies like Motorola file patents like raindrops and they have an army of lawyers to defend them. They rarely win if it goes all the way to court, but most companies do not have enough cash or wherewithal to stay in the fight till the end. Your best defense is a well documented, dated, written-in-ink engineering notebook. A notebook, if kept in the proper form, is a legal document and trumps a patent if the date in a notebook precedes the patent.

7 Your Work Environment and Staff

Create A Fun Environment Your People Enjoy

Every company has a culture. Different companies can run the gamut from a daily comedy routine to a boiler room slave shop. At ComNav we take the product seriously but not ourselves. I have tried to create an environment where jokes and hijinx are not only tolerated, they are encouraged.

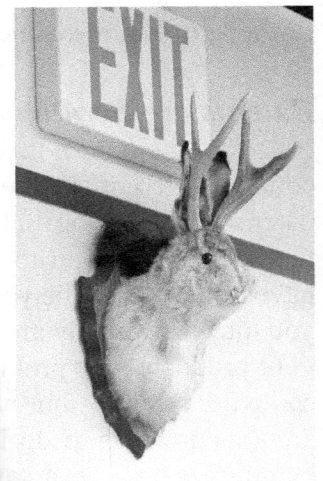

Shelly and Ray (general silliness)

The Nutty Factor

The most valuable asset any company can have is its people. If I had to name only one thing that sets ComNav apart from other companies, it's our *esprit de corps:* our company spirit. (Sometimes called *ethos.*) Who we know ourselves to be. We're fun-loving, hard-working, committed to excellence and nutty to our core. You don't have to be a little crazy to work here, but it helps!

Every company has struggles from day one of doing business. Looking back it's clear that it was going *through* the struggles *together* that created the ethos (the spirit) of this company.

ComNav's success is based on several key concepts that I believe and know to work.

The Sinatra Modus Operandi
We Do It *Our Way*

We meet the customer's timeframe and requirements with excellence, but we have fun and preserve our identity and integrity while doing it.

The Chutzpah Factor
We have the audacity and nerve to be ourselves while still meeting our customers' needs. Chutzpah (HOOTS-pah) is a Yiddish slang word meaning we are not afraid or embarrassed to do or say things that shock, surprise, or annoy other people. At ComNav we love finding unconventional approaches to the same old things.

The Churchill Mantra
We "Never, Never, Never, **Never** give up!"

The core of every company ought to be people. We see ourselves as a supportive family made up of individuals who are creative, caring, determined, responsible, resourceful, funloving, committed, adaptable, passionate and different (in a good way), with a can-do attitude that sees us through whatever challenges present themselves. We've all heard many business owners say, "The customer comes first." I think they missed the point. I believe *employees* should be first and customers should be *second*. Think about it. It's a little unconventional but it works for us.

ComNav people are talented and dependable in their own individual ways but when we are together, we can

accomplish anything. We're sort of like a salad: Each ingredient (person) enhances the flavor of the others. Working in that mix is refreshingly unconventional and makes coming to work very interesting.

A sense of the absurd also helps and provides comic relief for everyone. For example, the skeleton, *Bones.* When there is a job opening at ComNav, we position the skeleton in the vacant chair until we find someone to fill the opening. (This is the same skeleton that Lee asked me why I put it on the list of needed equipment and ordered it. He soon learned why we needed one.)

A few of the best and most remembered practical jokes over the years have included:

A kit box labeled *Chipmunk Wireless* with an actual dead chipmunk in the box. (That went over really well with the girls in assembly.)

Coating the eyecups of the inspection microscope with black lipstick so the inspector walked around for hours with raccoon eyes.

I chartered a boat for a whale watch and posted a $100 bounty on the best seasick photo.

One employee made coffee out of Diet Coke just to see everyone's reaction. He was then banned from ever making coffee again. (I think that's what he wanted in the first place.)

Leaving rubber dog poo in the middle of the production floor, then reaching down, picking it up, and taking a bite out of it.

Star Trek, Monty Python, Thomas Crapper, rubber chickens, tequila worms, stupid statues, all are part of the company's culture. For one example senior management (myself and my immediate staff), are called the bridge crew. All of the computers on our company network are named for Star Trek trivia. My business computer (the notebook I travel with), is named Tribble and my two design computers are named Kess and Porthos. Our server's name is Voyager. Also Monty Python features prominently in our voice mail system and when calling the company after hours and getting the automated answering system, callers are asked to press six if they'd like to discuss migrating coconuts. (More Monty Python on my right foot in the cover photo.) There have been numerous events over the years that have taken place all in an effort to create an *esprit de corps* to help ease tensions and bond people together.

Every year we have a combination birthday party/ stockholders meeting. I have rented stretch limos and taken everyone bowling. Every year I rent an entire snowpark for

an afternoon, shutdown the company and take everyone snow-tubing. I've chartered boats for whale-watching and evening music cruises, and bought tickets for everyone to go a Vince Neil concert and to many other events. Over the years I have worked very hard to create an environment where we look at each other as family. Anyone and everyone can and does walk into my office for an after-work beer and just to shoot the crap.

Get Good People; Get Them What They Need; Stay Out of Their Way

The quickest way to ruin morale is to constantly second-guess your people and go behind them, micro-managing their work. They have to be competent or you wouldn't have hired them in the first place! Supporting your people and giving them the authority along with the responsibility to 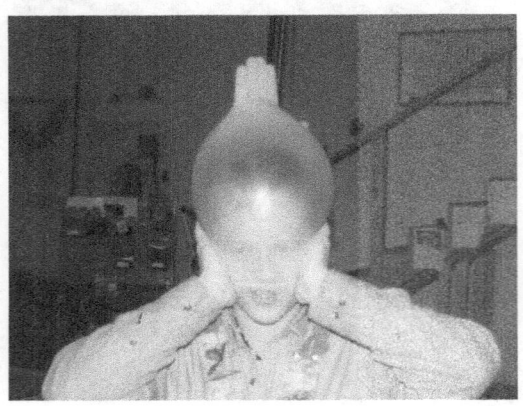 make decisions goes a long way in allowing you to delegate tasks with a minimum of follow-up. Delegation allows you to leverage your own strengths and accomplish much more than you can on your own. This is not to say that you tell your people to do something, then walk away and forget about it. You still need to follow-up, make sure they have the tools they need, that the task is going to accomplish your original intent, and your employees are comfortable making the decisions you asked them to make. It sounds obvious but in order to properly delegate, you need to know their strengths and weaknesses. You obviously don't ask an assembler to choose and purchase the proper $50,000 piece of equipment. By the same token you don't ask your VP of Engineering to select the toilet paper for the company restroom (though he may have a sensitive derriere and a strong opinion on the subject).

The worst thing you can do is go behind your employees and double-check every nuance of their decisions. You are only interested in the final result, or you should have done the task yourself. Most people actually like taking responsibility for their decisions and most people will even own up to their bad ones as long as they are working in a supportive environment. Brow-beating and demeaning bad decisions only make people reluctant to think for themselves in the future and it will eventually destroy their spirit. You want to maintain your staff's confidence not only in you but also in themselves.

Rituals, Rewards and Reprimands

Rituals bond people together through common experience. Good performance needs to be recognized and rewarded. Mistakes need to be acknowledged and corrected in a non-demeaning way.

Some of our items include annual company T-shirts with a silly slogan on the back, a worm ceremony as an initiation into management, rubber chickens for mistakes, get-out-of-chicken-free cards for Atta-Boys, and a Thomas Crapper award for a great idea.

The T-shirt slogan contest started after we were in business for a year and we were sitting around drinking one night. The subject of advertising came up and we were discussing how most advertising slogans sounded so professional and important and profound, but if you really spent time thinking about the slogan, it actually said absolutely nothing. Our first slogan was: *Where Quality and Innovation aren't just words; they are Big Words.*

After that first year we decided to turn the T-shirt slogan into a contest with a company-wide vote and all the employees contributing ideas for new slogans. There is no actual prize in the contest other than being able to tell everyone, "This year's slogan is mine." Over the years we have ended up with some self-deprecating slogans, some silly slogans, some profound slogans, and some downright stupid ones. We have them printed up every spring and distribute them to the employees and some close friends of the company at the annual birthday party/stockholders meeting. They have actually become a source of pride to the employees because they can display their seniority by which T-shirts they have.

Some examples of previous slogans include:

Able to ignore the Laws of Physics in a Single Beer

What do you mean? It worked when we shipped it.

We put the fun back in DysFUNction.

Impossible Solutions for Avoidable Problems

If our filters don't work, you hooked them up wrong.

A proud supporter of psychiatric work-release programs for 10 years

Where stupidity is a competitive advantage

Where the only thing stable are our filters

*ComNav Kennel and Daycare Center
Oh Yeah...We make filters too*

Maxwell's Equation:

$$\oint \vec{E} \cdot d\vec{A} = \frac{q}{\varepsilon_0}$$

$$\oint \vec{B} \cdot d\vec{A} = 0$$

$$\oint \vec{E} \cdot d\vec{s} = -\frac{d\Phi_B}{dt}$$

$$\oint \vec{B} \cdot d\vec{s} = \mu_0 i + \frac{1}{c^2}\frac{\partial}{\partial t}\int \vec{E} \cdot d\vec{A}$$

*Tagline: And you think **you** have problems?*

After the TelCom Crash we did this take-off on the Survivor TV show logo.

The T-shirt contest has become an important part of our company culture, a very popular annual ritual. About two months before the party, people get their creative juices flowing and start handing me T-shirt ideas. We usually end up with a couple dozen entries and I do filter out the more obscene and disgusting ones. After all these things are worn in public. Then everyone votes by picking their top three favorites. Then there is a runoff vote on the top five entries. Sometimes it gets pretty intense and some people will actually campaign for the slogan they like. It is all in good fun and provides us all with a common, binding experience.

The Worm Ceremony

The worm ceremony came about one night when I was at home drinking and watching Monty Python's Search for the Holy Grail. I had been trying to come up with a silly ceremony to initiate people who were being promoted into management.

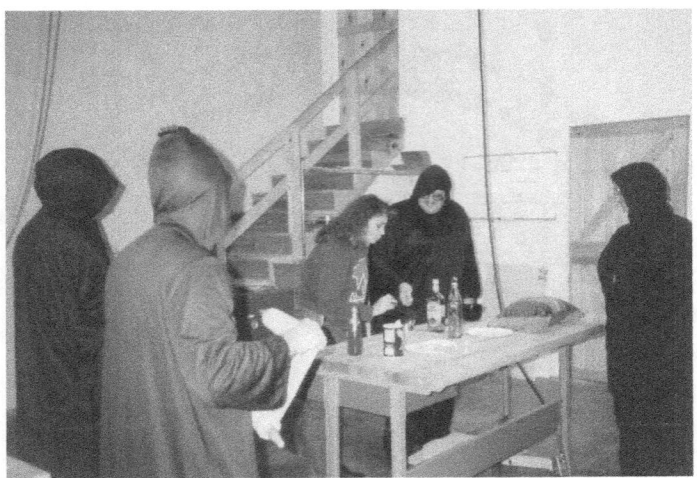

I received inspiration I needed from Brother Maynard quoting from the Sacred Book of Armaments describing the use of the Holy Hand Grenade. We were growing at such an exponential rate and supervisors were being promoted from the ranks after only working there for a month or two. If people showed a bit of ambition, and were conscientious about their jobs, and worked well with people, we made them supervisors. I wanted to come up with a silly ritual to acknowledge their promotion, so I came up with the Worm Ceremony. We still use it today when someone gets promoted to a position of responsibility. And yes, people actually do eat the tequila worm. In the 16 years we have been doing this, after several dozen worm ceremonies, no one has refused to eat the worm. The ceremony consists of myself and three previous worm eaters, dressed in black hooded robes, entering the room doing a silly Python-esque march and reading the ceremony from a script.

The Ceremony

The worm eaters march in doing the stupid worm march with each person taking his/her respective place. (Every third step the marchers do a little skip to the beat of bump, bump, ba-bump.) The Worm Crier takes his or her place at the near side of the table. The Worm Master takes his place behind the table. The Worm Drummer behind the Worm Master to the far side of the table, and the Courier of the Sacred Worm Bowl takes a place at the far side front of the table. Upon arriving at their respective positions the players stand stiffly silent for 10 seconds.

The Worm Crier speaks:

"*Hear Ye! Hear Ye! To all present:*

We are here to pay homage unto the worm. Within its body are contained the powers of mystical vision and the ability to view life from a slanteth position. These powers are much coveted and sought after by the management of ComNav Engineering and are required of those seeking high office within the company. From this day forward all managers of ComNav Engineering must be worm eaters, and only worm eaters can be managers. In order to become a manager one must eat the worm. Only after eating the worm can one become a manager. Upon eating the worm one is eligible to become a worm eater and manage the company. ComNav Engineering is a company run by worm eaters who have eaten the worm.

To become a senior manager one must not only eat the worm, but bite the worm in half prior to its consumption. Upon biting the worm in half, those wishing to become senior managers must hold half the worm aloft for all to see. Following the pubic display of half the worm the aforementioned worm-half must be eaten, chewing being at the option of the individual worm eater.

The worm shall not be expelled from the worm eater's body prematurely. The worm must not be spitith out. Whosoever shall spitith out the worm shall be condemned to clean the men's bathroom for a period of one month. Nor must the worm be expelled by the involuntary blowing of chunks, for the chunk-blower shall be deemed unworthy of high position.

Upon the worm's being eaten by those seeking to attain high office, the event shall be celebrated by those present with the congratulatory golf clap. Should anyone present speaketh the words, "Ooooh, gross," that person shall be condemned to cleaning the men's bathroom one time.

The Worm Master has prepared the first worm and speaks:
"For whom does the worm call?"

After holding the worm to his ear to hear the name of the new worm-eater, the Worm Master speaks:
"The worm calleth: (name of worm-eater)."

(During the eating of the worm the worm master prepareth the next worm.)

(The worm master has prepared the next worm.)

Worm Crier:
"Worm Master, is the next worm ready?"

Worm Master:
"The next worm is ready!"

Worm Crier:
"Worm Master, for whom does the worm call?"

(After holding the worm to his ear to hear the name of the new worm-eater, the worm master speaks):
Worm Master:
"The worm calleth: (name of worm eater)"

This cycle continues until all worms have been eaten.
After the last worm has been eaten the Worm Crier speaks:
"Now we shall dance to celebrate the transfer of the worm's mystical powers into the management of ComNav Engineering."

The music master starts the CD of *Safety Dance by Men without Hats a*nd the worm eaters along with everyone else dance in a line around the company, as stupidly as possible.

End of Ceremony

Remember: This is not meant to be taken seriously. Anything that can be done to make the event even more ridiculous is strongly encouraged.

Over the years the worm ceremony has proven to be very popular with the staff. It not only acknowledges the new supervisors' advancement, but also shows the managers' participating in the ceremony in a lighthearted fashion. It also works wonders to remove the us-versus-them attitude so prevalent in many companies. With the managers dressed up in silly robes, doing a stupid march, and participating in a ridiculous ceremony, they become more approachable on a day-to-day basis, the lines of communication in the company are greatly enhanced, and management/worker friction is greatly reduced.

Rubber Chickens

Rubber chickens also play an important role at ComNav Engineering. When an employee makes a minor mistake, no one gets chewed out or reprimanded, but he or she receives a rubber chicken. The chicken stays with the individual until someone else screws up, which is usually only a couple of days. The main thing the chicken accomplishes is to generate peer pressure to do a good job with an eye toward quality. No one likes to receive a chicken, but eveyone wants to give one.

Therefore everyone of the employees from top management down to the newest hire is on the lookout for mistakes. They are found quickly and corrected immediately.

Though it sounds silly and juvenile, giving rubber chickens is one of the reasons ComNav has achieved its reputation in the marketplace of providing top quality components, and we have very few returns. No one is immune; if I screw up on a design or production paperwork, it is guaranteed there will be a procession to my office with chicken in hand. In addition to handing out rubber chickens internally, the company also hands them out to vendors. If a vendor screws up, a rubber chicken is sent along with the bad parts and a copy of the chicken clause of ComNav's quality manual. (Yes, we have actually formalized rubber chickens in our ISO 9000 quality system.) ComNav passes its audit every year. We just have to show the ISO auditor our formal chicken file, showing to whom and why we sent out chickens that year. The formal vendor chicken policy states that, after three chickens, the vendor gets re-evaluated and if necessary, the company finds a new vendor.

On the other side of the coin, if an employee does a good job, or finds a pending mistake before it becomes serious, or in other words, does something deserving of an Atta-Boy, the company presents a *Get-Out-Of-Chicken-Free-Card*. This entitles the recipient to one chicken-free screw-up. These cards are handed out by line supervisors and are only available to the actual hands-on workers.

Senior management is not entitled to receive any *Get-Out-of-Chicken-Free-Cards*. They must take their chicken like a man or woman since their mistakes are generally more expensive and have larger consequences.

For coming up with a really great idea or solving a tough problem or coming up with a way to save the company a significant amount of money, the company has an award above and beyond the Get-Out-of-Chicken-Free-Card: the much - coveted Crapper Award. This award is given along with a $100 bill to the deserving individual. The award is in honor of Thomas Crapper, an inventor who created the most important technology used in the modern era: the flush toilet. No more going outdoors to the outhouse in the middle of January and freezing your butt cheeks to the seat. So to honor his memory, ComNav has created this award for extreme creativity. In addition to the Crapper Award, we also take the first Monday in March as a company holiday, known as Crapper Day, to further honor this great inventor.

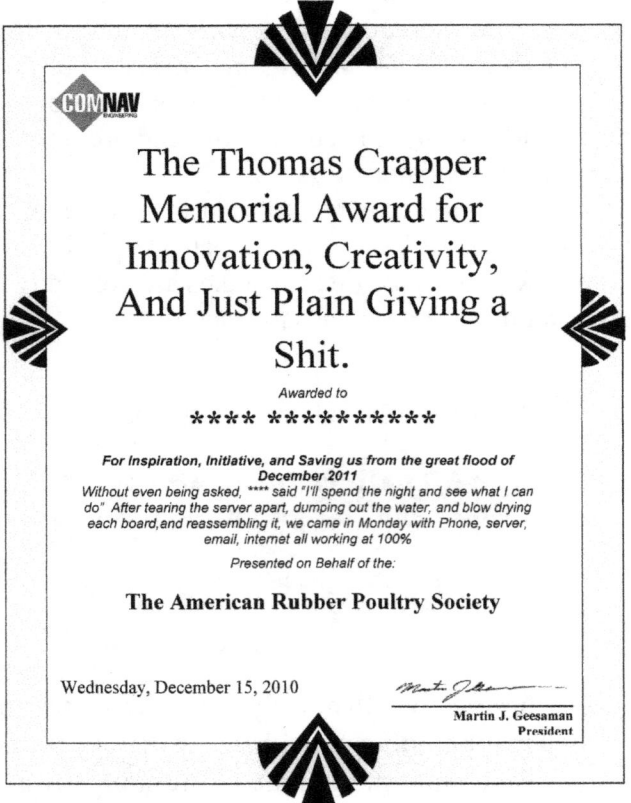

(The name of the recipient has been removed to protect his anonymity and so I don't have to pay him a residual.)

8 External Associates

Your Sales reps Are Your Face to the Customer

Depending on who you talk to, some people consider reps essential and absolutely necessary to do busienss, and others consider them parasites. In reality they can be both; it all depends on how you structure yoru rep agreement. As I mentioned previously my rep agreement is based on design-wins and we do not pay commission based on product shipped to a territory.

To some reps this is unacceptable; they want to be able to collect commission checks on everything shipped into their territory. This allows them to sit on their butts and provide no value added to the transaction but still collect commission. They will justify it by saying you are new to the territory and will require a lot of missionary work, and there will be no cash flow to support it. Actually this is totally true and I agree with this set of facts. But my attitude is: that is the nature of the rep business and if that is an issue with you, then why did you become a rep in the first place?

I can almost guarantee that if you cave and agree even to split commissions, a year later you will have paid tens of thousands of dollars and you will not get a single new order. When you really think about the missionary aspect of opening a new territory, that is exactly why I only pay on design wins. Most companies, especially big ones, have distinct design centers and production centers. For example the design center could be in Silicon Valley and the production is built on the other side of the country. The rep who did all the missionary work to get you designed in deserves to reap the fruits of his effort. The man in the territory where production is built does nothing but receive the order and fax it. Sometimes there are reasons to split commission and also compensate the production rep. This is usually an issue in foreign countries where the local rep handles the importing and acts as translator or cultural liaison.

Vendors Are Your Strength

It is imperative that you maintain close symbiotic relationships with your vendors and treat them like friends and family. They can save your butt during the bad times. Yeah, we all want the best price for raw materials. But finding good quality, fair-priced vendors who deliver in a timely manner most of the time should be your top priority right from the beginning. Once found don't force them to bid for jobs.

Obviously this only works with honest vendors but you will be able to identify the weasels early and move on. If you cultivate the relationship and become close drinking buddies, you can partner and form strong bonding relationships that will help both of you in the longterm. When you are in bad shape, they will carry you longer than normal. If they need help, pay your invoices immediately or in advance. When you are running strong, they get a steady cash flow. When they are running strong, they will always find a way to squeeze you in.

A good example from our past that shows the value of a strong vendor relationship is how our ceramic vendor in Japan helped us survive the tech-bubble burst. As I've mentioned we are primarily known as a ceramic filter supplier, so even in slow times we consume a lot of ceramic. The type we use most is a TEM resonator which has a square cross-section and a length determined by the frequency required. It has a hole through the center and is completely coated with silver. Our supplier in Japan makes the best that we have found in terms of quality and consistency. We never shop them. We use so much that if we went out of business it would be a major blow to our Japanese friends. The president of the company (who speaks minimal English), asked his U.S. sales manager to ask me if they could help us out. He invited me over to Japan to discuss it. To make a long story short he gave me $100,000 on a handshake. We wrote up an agreement that was less than a half-page describing the agreed upon payment terms, interest, and the exchange rate, yen to dollars. The agreement wasn't even a contract; it was just to remind us what we agreed to. ComNav did well enough, fast enough and I was able to pay it off in half the time. I flew over to Japan to personally hand him the final check and thank him for his help. Our relationship is more like family than business associates.

Accountants, Bankers and Lawyers, "Oh My!"

Every business needs outside professional help. I will not do my payroll in-house because of the temptation to skim payroll taxes. (Oh, we can make it up next month.) That doesn't fly. The IRS does not believe in next month. A good corporate attorney doesn't just file paperwork, he is a friend and a good advisor and sounding board. A good accountant will help you minimize your tax load and keep you running above board. Most bankers are weasels. Avoid them at all cost. When you don't need them they will kiss your butt and skim your profits. When you do need them, they will pull the rug out from under you. But lately I have found some good bankers that I consider good friends and they deal honestly and straight forward. My bad experience has been with big banks, so my advice about bankers would be to find one that is right-sized for your business, and as small as possible. Smaller banks are much easier to work with.

We have all heard lawyer jokes and how lawyers are the bottom of the professional food chain, but I can attest that there are many rungs on the ladder below lawyers. Business brokers, headhunters and of course, some bankers, just to name a few. A good corporate attorney is worth his weight in gold in helping navigate the legal issues involved in running a company.

My corporate attorney is not only my lawyer, he is a valued advisor and friend. He also owns a few shares of stock in the company. He works for one of the larger law firms here and has attorneys in his firm who specialize in import-export law, labor law, contract law, collections and pretty much any kind of mess I find myself in at the time. So my man handles the bulk of my legal needs, but when I get into some esoteric area that is not his specialty, he calls in other resources as necessary. He is also a great fit with the company and appreciates our sense of humor, fitting right in with the rest of us. In fact when he performed my wedding ceremony, he did so wearing a Viking helmet.

My accountant is another valued asset. Maintaining the corporate books in proper order, setting up transactions properly, minimizing taxes, these are all issues that contain extreme subtleties that require outside expertise, even for someone with an MBA. The tax laws change so rapidly that it's impossible to keep current and still have time to actually run a company. Besides, tax law is no Clancy novel; I can barely get through one paragraph without my attention drifting to something more interesting like how fast my grass is growing. I have worked with the same accountant from the days when ComNav was a basement company, so we have an excellent history and she knows my priorities without my having to spend hours in her office going over endless financial transactions. Between her and my in-house business manager, I can stay away from numbers with dollar signs as much as possible. I'll do strategic forecasting, the occasional cash flow analysis, and some financial forecasting, but the day-to-day accounting details I avoid like the plague.

Occasionally you have to borrow money to expand, buy equipment, or just survive. This is when you are forced to deal with bankers and finance companies. Bankers are a necessary evil, but never let them get enough leverage on you to cause you damage. Pay them off as soon as possible.

Equipment financers are actually more helpful and reliable than classic bankers. You go into the transaction knowing exactly what to expect and as long as you are making your payments in a timely manner they will leave you alone. Bankers (especially from big banks), want quarterly financial reports, annual audits, and are looking over your shoulder for the slightest hint of trouble. As soon as something makes them nervous, they freak out, call your loans, shut down your credit line, and demand payment immediately. You will get a call from your friendly banker (as he sticks his knife in your heart), saying, "It's not personal; it's just business." Bottom line: Never, never, ever sign a loan with financial contingencies and ratio requirements. Even if it comes down to closing day and they are slipped in at the last minute, get up from the table, walk away and find another bank. In the long run you will be better off even with the delay in obtaining financing.

Currently I use a credit union. Credit unions are a lot like banks except they are owned by the depositors and are usually limited to their local markets. Since they are so small, you can pick up the phone and set up a lunch with your personal account rep and it's the same person you had lunch with two years ago. As a result you form more of a trusting personal relationship than just an account number that gets transferred to an account manager three states away whom you've never met.

So when it comes to banks I much prefer a small town local bank or credit union than a big mega bank that promises you the moon. To the big bank you are a number; to a small bank you are not just a customer, you're someone they know. If your lending needs go beyond your little bank's comfort level, then most likely they will help pull in a partner bank and you can still get the level of financing you need and maintain your local contacts. In my experience this personal relationship is much more important than a one-stop-shop mega bank that's *too big to fail.*

Not all weasels are slicky boys and, to be fair, not all slicky boys are weasels. The difference between slicky boys and weasels is that weasels are impressed with themselves and the slicky boys go out of their way to impress you. You always want to do business with people you trust who can make quick decisions.

Weasels are out to just suck your cashflow. They are the consultants that drop by unannounced and pretend to be your best friend, the phone bank caller trying to sell you the next big penny stock, landlords who don't return deposit checks...I think you get the picture. In general they are people who initially say they have your best interests at heart but after they suck you in, they drop all pretense of integrity and really only want your cash.

Slicky boys are suit-wearing, very stiff, corporate men

who try to come off as being the consummate professional. They have all the solutions to problems you never even knew you had. After all you are just a lowly entremaneur and they are M.B.A. graduates. They have never actually run a business but they wrote plenty of papers about it in school. They typically have to have three committee meetings to determine how many sheets of toilet paper to use to wipe their butts.

Headhunters, Consultants, Brokers and Other Parasites

Once your company is up and running, there will be an endless parade of parasites trying to suck your cash. I never do business with a coldcaller. If I need something I shop for it myself. Stockbrokers, M&A men, language interpreters, financing, training programs, equipment jobbers: the types of cold calls are endless. Not only are they out to suck your cash, they also steal your time. Some of these people will not get off the phone. It has become a game with our receptionist to ferret out these calls and cut them off. We even have one extension on our phone system with a snippy message that we transfer them to. If they do get through, I show no mercy. They are wasting my time and I am usually busy. If they wake me up from a nap, I will be especially brutal. They are worse than telemarketing calls because they will do a little bit of research and have just enough information to make you think you either know them or they are a real customer or vendor. By the time you realize it's a cold call they have used up five or ten minutes of your time. No need to be nice; they do not deserve courtesy, especially the scammers.

Headhunters are a special case because they can cause serious damage to your company and engineer a brain-drain. Once you hire someone through a headhunter, they are like cockroaches; you cannot get them out of your company. they could care less about your busienss or your peoples' careers. They are pimps that make money by shopping people around. They work by doing follow-up calls with the person they placed and then casually ask the names of other people in your company and start trying to prospect them. Hopefully you have created an environment where your people are content.

But even when a headhunter starts blowing smoke up people's butts about doubling their salaries, people get sucked in. Then the headhunter will start laying guilt trips about all the work he has done on their behalf and a sense of obligation sets in. I have been hired for jobs through headhunters and it made me feel slimy. Then after I took the job, they were relentless trying to get the names of my coworkers. Not all headhunters are weasels, but the few that aren't are so rare it's a statistical anomaly.

The old saying about consultants is that they come in, create total chaos and then leave and everyone left is holding the bag of crap they left behind. That is not to say that some consultants cannot be a great asset. We use benefit consultants, 401K consultants, and of course, I always get advice from our corporate attorneys.

The men who show up at your door and send the unsolicited e-mail clamoring to show you a new and improved way of doing business and use such words as synergy, paradigm shift, out of the box thinking, yada-yada, should be shown to the door immediately and not welcomed back.

Real estate brokers are a necessary evil; business brokers, on the other hand, are generally weasels. When the time comes to sell your company, it is very hard to find a decent business broker. But ask around. Check out his/her catalog of previous deals and talk to the owners. If they say they can't give out that information and start talking confidentiality, cut them loose Obviously they are hiding something. If they ask for a retainer or want to charge a similar fee, cut them loose.

We worked with one business brokerage firm who sucked us in when we were flying high. We paid them a bunch of cash; they sent us a book; and we never heard from them again. A year later we heard the entire senior staff was indicted. So be careful. These guys can be sharks, so definitely do your due diligence on them.

When it is time to sell your business, you will definitely get the highest price from someone in your industry, especially a public company, since they can finance the sale by issuing shares and don't have to come up with a lot of cash. Someone in your industry (especially if you have an engineering company), will recognize the value of your design library. A portfolio/holding company is just looking for net income and could care less about the intangibles because they don't understand them.

SCAR WARS: Battle #9

Jeff Denyer is the de facto fix-it guy around here. He's very mechanically inclined and can usually fix anything.

When one of the big drying ovens went out on us, Jeff was trying to fix it.

Something gave way inside and a big flash of fire came bursting out. When it blew, our quality manager landed on his butt.

We still joke about Jeff's having a tendency to set people on fire.

9 Management
Remember You Are the Boss

There is nothing wrong about gathering opinions and getting a consensus, but always remember this: Your business is not a democracy; it is a benevolent dictatorship. In addition most people feel safe and secure with a strong confident leader. If the boss is wishy-washy or easily manipulated it will ultimately create a toxic political environment. Every one of your employees, whether being malicious or not, will try to seek advantage, special privilege or status. It's just human nature: Everyone thinks he or she is special. If you are confident, direct, focused and fair, your employees will have respect for you and honor your wishes and feel treated in an equitable manner. This doesn't mean you have to force your opinion on everyone and demand that no one question your authority. But once a decision is made you must follow through on it, unless it becomes obvious it is wrong. In fact my employees joke about me by saying, "Often wrong; never in doubt." Sometimes I am stubborn, but I am not a jerk about it. When I am occasionally proven wrong I take the ribbing and jokes in stride. I am not trying to be omnipotent (though I joke that I am); I am providing unconfused and confident direction for our efforts, and occasionally I screw up. For example: Once I spent almost $20K on a custom machine to try and automate our coating process. It was a dismal failure. To this day when I come up with a sketchy idea, someone always asks, "This isn't going to be another of Marty's Follies, is it?"

The main thing to keep in mind is your entire financial future and all of your assets are tied to the company. You can't just wake up one morning and say, I don't like this. I am going to get another job. (Of course, if you do wake up thinking that, it is probably time to start looking at selling out anyway.) You are not only financially bound, you are also legally bound. It's not your employees' property that's being used as collateral, and they can leave anytime they want. Your signature is on all the documents, so you are the captain and the captain goes down with the ship. In the case of severe cash flow problems, payroll doesn't go on their personal credit cards, it goes on yours. The company is your lifeline, but you are also the company's lifeline. So ask for their opinion, ask for their advice, but ultimately the decision must be yours. If anyone constantly questions your authority, or complains about your decisions, get rid of him or her because that person is most likely trying to undermine you behind your back.

Learn from Your Mistakes and Let Them Go

When we initially grew really fast due to the Telecom bubble I invested over $150K in an empty building to convert it into a manufacturing facility. We continued to grow and quickly outgrew that facility. I needed to find more space just to keep up with our current capacity. In addition the company was in two buildings three miles apart, which created communication problems. I then came across an abandoned ice cream plant that was currently being renovated. I leased 25,000 square feet, worked with the developer and invested another $400,000 to make it suitable for our manufacturing processes and also to pay riggers to move the company. I could have bought and added onto the initial building, but the landlord was a total weasel, and I didn't have the time to interrupt production for the disruption the rehab would have caused.

As I have mentioned already, right after we moved into the ice cream plant, the bottom fell out of the market. Just to survive I had to abandon that project and move back to our original space. In total I had to walk away from $550,000 in order to save the company. Pretty much all my profit for those two wild-ride years was gone in a flash, just so I could save the company. But I did it and I have no regrets. If I hadn't walked away but had kept trying to fix it, my company would have followed my customers to the wonderful world of Chapter 7.

Sometimes You Have to Be an Obnoxious Jerk; Other Times It's Just Fun

One thing that aggravates me more than anything else is working with a customer through the design and prototype stage and then once all the hard work is done, they shop me on price. So I created the Dickhead clause. This is invoked when I have proven the design and have delivered prototypes and some production quantity and I give the customer the price and they come back and say my competitor can do it for less. Rarely do I cave on price. My pricing is fair and competitive, and usually in these cases the competitor is trying to drive me away from the customer. The Dickhead clause states that if you drop me on price and the competitor can't deliver and you come back to me, it is an automatic 25% increase in price. Customers tell me, "You can't do that!" and I say, "Yes, I can, because I am a Dickhead." I have saved six-figure purchase orders with the Dickhead clause and royally frustrated my competitors. It's a win-win!

Another time I got into a fight with a landlord who refused to return a deposit, even though I spent $150,000 in upgrades to his building. We ended up in small claims court. His argument was that I didn't leave the building in the same condition I found it. My attorney's response was that the situation could easily be remedied with a couple sticks of dynamite. I had put in new restrooms, added a second floor, upgraded the wiring, and painted the place. It turned out he was running a mini Ponzi scheme and had spent my deposit to cover something else and hadn't put it into an escrow account as he was legally required to do. I took him to court and, at that point, I didn't care if I paid my attorney more than the lost deposit amount. I just wanted to make him miserable. In fact I didn't even go to court; I sent one of my accounting clerks as a further insult to let him know he was not worthy of my time.

Immature, yes. Childish, yes. Good business sense, no. Gesture of futility, yes. But, hey. Did we give up when the Germans bombed Pearl Harbor? (Paraphrased from the movie *Animal House*.)

Pushovers Get Pushed Over

Whether it is in your home business community, your industry, with your vendors, your sales reps, or your customers, if you get a reputation as a pushover, you will be pushed over. Occasionally you have to cave. That is part of negotiations. But you can never allow yourself to be pushed into a bad decision where you are left holding the dirty end of the stick. You must make money on every job. You have to pay fair prices on products and services; you do not want to be forced into long-term contracts; and you cannot let employees browbeat you into bad personnel decisions.

Make Embezzlement As Difficult As Possible

We've all heard many news stories about kindly-looking grandmotherly bookkeepers being led away in handcuffs for stealing tens or hundreds of thousands of dollars from their employers. Having access to a company's cash is an incredible temptation.

It is very easy for your bookkeeper to write him/herself a check and go back and make a change in your accounting system to make the check reflect a real vendor. Short of a full audit on both your own and your vendor's books, it is very difficult to track unless it's an obvious entry. So other than doing a security clearance level background check on your bookkeeper or handling all the money yourself, how do you avoid this problem?

The easiest way is to not allow the same person who writes the checks to also sign them and vice-versa. You do need to have multiple signatories so you can go on vacation. In my company it's my executive VP, my production manager and myself.

I usually do all the signing so I can see where the cash is going. But when I am on vacation or a sales trip, I have two other people whom I trust take care of it for me. However the people authorized to sign checks are not authorized to write them. The only person with both authorities is myself. But even then I always check with accounting before I write a check, especially a large one, to make sure the cash isn't earmarked for something else.

It's a shame we have to take these kinds of precautions but it is better to be safe than sorry.

Your Negotiation Strength Is Proportional to What You Are Willing to Lose

If you are willing to go into an all-or-nothing negotiation, you will have maximum flexibility and negotiate from a position of strength. Basically you don't care, so you really have nothing to lose. This situation occurs more often than you'd think. If a customer is trying to shove a price down your throat that you know will be a money-loser, or a landlord is trying to force you into a ten-year-lease, or a supplier is giving you a ridiculously high price, walk away. There are other customers, other properties, and other suppliers.

Don't Get Too Bogged Down in Details

Any company of more than two or three people has thousands of minute details that have to be addressed every day. If you tried to manage everything yourself, you'd go crazy and never actually accomplish anything. I keep a few basic facts in my head: cash on hand, monthly bookings and shipments, the size of payroll, overview type details.

I paint broad brushstrokes of what I want to accomplish and let my staff fill in the details. In order for this to work, you have to delegate the authority as well as the responsibility and give your staff the freedom to screw up. Yes they do screw up occasionally but, unless it was malicious or completely unethical, I just hand out a rubber chicken and then move on.

Take a Motley Moment

Occasionally the tension will build, or there are so many details coming at you that you get to the point where you think you are going to explode. You need to disconnect and reset your attitude. I do this by going into my office, kicking back in my chair, closing my eyes and blasting *Motley Crue* on my stereo. It is kind of a joke around the company when it's playing and my employees tell each other,"Leave him alone; he's taking a Motley Moment."

Also you need to identify your times of peak efficiency and make your big decisions and do your complex tasks then. For me it is in the morning before lunch. I am fired up on about five cups of coffee and I can get an incredible amount of work done in a short period of time. After lunch (typically between one and three in the afternoon), I am useless, so I do my brain-dead activities then: take a Motley Moment, surf the web, or take a nap.

Your Primary Job Is Strategic Planning and Conflict Resolution

Your people crave leadership from you. It's not just so they can abrogate responsibility and be able to say, "Well, that's what you told me to do." There is some of that but very little. It's because people like to be working toward something and striving for some goal. It is your job to provide that goal. It must be reasonable. If you are currently shipping $200,000 per month and then tell your production manager you want to ship $400,000 next month, that is just stupid. Telling your sales manager to double sales next quarter is just as bad. Some aberration may occur, and he may do it, but don't expect it and hold him or the rest your staff accountable to an unattainable goal.

Set rational, reasonable, moderately increasing thresholds of expectation. A company that is growing at a manageable rate is a happy company. some of your people may not understand the complexities of business, but they know when the business is growing and they have job security. People who feel secure in their jobs are content, productive and motivated. Your function is to develop long-term strategies that keep the company stable and growing.

Anytime you get more than one person in a room, there will be politics. We all say we hate politics but it is a fact of life. The ups and downs of conflict and compromise are exactly how we all get along and get things done. A small company is a lot like a family where we all know one another both professionally and personally. So there will always be sibling rivalry. One of the biggest problems with managing conflict is that, as the boss, you rarely get the entire story. But no matter what, you can never take sides. Usually getting people together face-to-face to talk out their differences will solve the problem or at the very least cool it off. It can be very uncomfortable, because you feel close to all parties involved and you don't want anyone's feelings hurt. But occasionally you have to play Dr. Phil and hold a mirror up to people

All companies have good times and bad times. You have to be very careful during the good times that you don't get caught up in the moment, and start spending cash extravagantly. Unless you can pay for that new Ferrari out of petty cash, don't do it. Things can change tomorrow: market crash, terroriest attack, hurricane. Any multitude of things can affect your business and cause a dramatic slow down. During the bad times, remember there is always tomorrow and things can change for the better just about as fast as they can for the worse. So fight through it.

> **SCAR WARS: Battle #10**
>
> Then there was the ultrasonic incident. We were trying to clean some wires and couldn't get the flux off no matter what we tried. We had been using some chemical cleaner that was not supposed to be put into the ultrasonic but into a soaking bath instead. On my way out the door I had said, "Maybe we should put it in the ultrasonic." It was an explosion waiting to happen. It didn't actually explode but I fast realized I need to be careful with sarcastic comments when I am frustrated.

10 The Staff
Wanted: An Open Mind and a Sense of Humor

Obviously ComNav isn't interested in hiring someone who has no sense of humor. We take people off the streets when we recognize their talents and then we move them up through the ranks. We have a sixth sense about where people are coming from. For example two machinists apply for a job. One is good at producing a lot in a hurry. One is good at precision work. ComNav needs them both. And they are both happy and productive.

We want an open mind and a good sense of humor. We wouldn't be interested in hiring someone who is strongly opinionated or someone who had worked at another filter company for years. We also look for moderate mechanical ability. We do background checks. Minor stuff doesn't bother us. We go by gut feeling and we get it wrong about 50% of the time. We don't do a lot of professional hires. We prefer to promote from within.

Once we needed to hire and unemployment was at 4%. We had trouble finding workers. We contacted Catholic Charities to see if they had any leads for us. They asked if we would be willing to give refugees a try. We said sure and hired 10 to 12 of them. I was amazed at how quickly they picked up on things and how quickly they learned. At that time we were running two shifts for coating the resonators. I came in very late one night when we were running two shifts and I tripped over two workers who were doing their evening prayers in the dark. They didn't get upset and we still laugh about it to this day.

Hiring workers isn't easy, especially at ComNav. We are looking more for a personality type than a skill set. Skills can be taught but attitude is ingrained. When we feel it's right, we go ahead with the hire. Sometimes we mess up and the person doesn't work out. With the minimal supervision and the sink-or-swim training technique we use, some people just don't work in this environment. We typically have 50-60 percent success rate on new hires. On the 40-50 percent who don't make it, it is unusally their own decision. Numerous times we have had new hires go to lunch and just not come back. I am sure as they leave they are thinking to themselves, "These people are nuts!"

ComNav's Three-tier Probation Period

First: If the hiree proves to be a jerk, we know it within 30 days and he or she is fired. This rarely occurs and the person must be pretty disruptive for this to happen.

Second: The basic competency period lasts for three months. Its purpose is to see if the probationer has learned the required skills. If the individual is really quick and comes up to speed fast, the supervisor can shorten this period at his or her option.

Third: At the end of the first year you are probably going to stay around. Benefits kick in and you become a member of the ComNav family. This is the period known as *Welcome to the Family!*

One of our first employment ads

In Their Own Words...

Tomi (Thomasina) Auger
Quality Assistant, Seven years

In 1999 I answered a ComNav ad in the paper because one of my teachers at adult education saw it and thought I'd be a good fit for the job they were offering. My first impression of the company was that it was corny, but I liked it! During the interview Marty began explaining MHz (megahertz) and Ghz (gigahertz) to me. It piqued my curiosity. I was impressed with the family orientation and laid-back atmosphere. I really wanted that job!

For the next few weeks I kept calling the company to find out if anyone else had interviewed and what were my chances of getting the job. Marty began wondering if I was a bunny-boiler (a stalker)! I came back and talked with him, saying I thought I could be an asset to the company and that I wanted to learn about frequencies. He said he'd give me a try but it would be sink or swim. He also promised, "We'll pull you up before you drown." At that time my daughter was 14 and my son was two. I respected the fact that Marty was a single dad raising his kids mostly by himself while running his own very busy company. He was able to relate to those of us with families and children.

After the first six months I became manager for the sales department, something I really liked. (Yes, I had to eat the worm!) Marty was right: It was sink or swim! But he always pulled me up by the ponytail as he had promised. We are like a big family here and I look up to him as a big brother. We had two buildings at that time with around 100 employees and business was really booming. Eventually things slowed down and we had to lay people off. Those of us who were left went out for sushi and sake to drown our sadness over the layoffs. The company got smaller, leaner. Marty's motto became: *Keep it small. Keep it all.*

I left the company in 2005 because I had met my knight in shining armor and decided it was time to move on. I took another job but the relationship with coworkers was missing. Then Shelly called to tell me about a job opening on the production floor for less pay. If I wanted it they would grandfather me in for the time I had worked there before. It wasn't a hard decision to make. I would rather make less money and be happy. So I came back. It was like coming home.

What makes ComNav different is the close relationship between Marty and each of his employees. We truly are family. No one is a number; we are friends.

Pat Foss
Drafting (formerly IT), 16 years

I think I hold the record for longevity, except for Marty. I began working here the same month the company started, June 1996. I came in for an interview and they had set up a drafting station and a skeleton was sitting in the chair. It was explained that by putting the skeleton in the chair they believed the right person would show up almost immediately. At that point I realized this was not a normal company.

My first job was IT and drafting. I also chipped in where needed and did some repair and carpentry work. (Any excuse to get away from the computer and play with my power tools.) There is no It's-not-my-job" attitude here. Everyone does whatever is needed. I greatly enjoy the challenge and the variety ComNav provides. In all my previous jobs I got bored and left after two years. I've been at ComNav for over 16 years. Now I do drafting exclusively. The electronic engineers design a circuit diagram and tell me the basic parameters of the package it has to go into. I figure out the components and the physical layout and create the drawings we send out to vendors. I had earned three degrees from Southern Maine Technical College: electronics, computer technology, and technical graphical illustration. One day I was filling out an application and copying my resume at the SMTC Career Center. I overheard the secretary taking a call from Marty outlining the job available. I followed up, was interviewed and was hired. It was pretty much what I was looking for in IT. Right now I have my own office and enough variation to keep me from getting bored. I really like not wearing a tie to work! At one point I was putting in a lot of extra time developing a web page for ComNav even though Marty didn't think we needed one. I thought we did. He appreciated the time I was putting in so he gave me a raise and made me a salaried employee so I could work flexible hours.

Shelly Craft
Production Manager, 16 years

I had no background for this job. They were looking for microwave assemblers and I thought we were going to be putting microwave ovens together! After my tour of the company, I understood what the work involved. I had only a high school diploma, but I had drive and I wouldn't give up. I wasn't hired right away but when they did call me I started out in the coating lab. I'm one of only three people who know the secret ingredients to coating.

My next job was in the chip and wire lab where I was the only person there. I assembled chip and wire filters, hand-wound coils, and placed substrate for about four years. Sometimes I spent all night at the company—just me and my chip and wire. I wasn't required to do that; I chose to do it. It was quiet at night and I enjoyed the work.

In 2004 I was promoted to production manager, the

job I still have. I love my job because it's challenging and personally fulfilling. This place is like another family to me! At holidays we do potluck dinners; we also go on outings as a company and the families come along. We have this great family feeling because Marty has always driven into us that family comes first. I think part of the company's success is due to Marty's being driven and a go-getter. He always gives his all to whatever he's doing. And he doesn't back down from a challenge.

Once when I went on vacation, Marty and Kirk and Shawn ran the production for me. When I came back I went into Marty's office and there stood all three of them in a row, wearing protective cups over their pants! They didn't hit the production numbers and thought I would be unhappy with how they had run the production floor! (I was not unhappy at all!) I just can't imagine working anyplace else!

Kirk Riley
Vice President of Engineering, 15 years

In 1996 in my senior year at UMaine in Orono, I was looking for only a summer job because after earning my BS, I planned to immediately earn my Masters. My adviser at UMaine knew about ComNav and I ended up in a job interview with Marty. The conversation went something like this:"So you tailored your resume to this position?"
"Yeah."
"Would you like a scotch or a beer?"
"Sure. Alright."
"You can start tomorrow."
I worked summers until I completed all my degree work. For one year I worked for a different company after completing my Masters. I didn't enjoy the anonymity and lack of impact after working in a small company, so I returned to ComNav full-time, despite a cut in salary. Just before the

dot-com crash, I decided to get a PhD in computer engineering from Purdue. The timing worked out, as I left soon after the crash when ComNav needed to downsize. After those five years at Purdue, I returned. Now I do some of the initial quoting for jobs and take things from the theoretical stage to the actual components. The drafting department reports to me and the technicians also report to me. I'm involved in some of the reviewing, and also work with production on problem solving."

Shawn White
Engineering Assistant, 16 years

I worked with Marty at Control Devices. He was head of the coaxial department there. It was a small crew but we all worked well together. Even though it was a small department we had the resources of GTE and Marty was always coming up with crazy ideas to do things better. Some worked and others didn't. One thing for sure is if you saw Marty coming we all hid our tools, because he always seemed to walk away with something that wasn't his. We didn't talk too often in those days because he always had a million things and ideas bouncing around in his head. One of his favorite sayings is, "I'm a legend in my own mind."

Eventually I left Control Devices and moved out of state and when I came back to Maine I saw Marty at a local store. He asked me if I wanted a job. I said yes, and the following week I was employed at ComNav Engineering. That was 16 years ago.

Now I tune filters in the tuning lab, which means I tune the filter's resonances to certain specifications. A filter manipulates a certain frequency band in an RF system. Our customers ask for a certain frequency with a variety of other specifications and I try to make it work. I also build filters but I like tuning them better because it feels good to know the stuff I do tune is being sent around the world and I had an important part in making technology happen.

I like the atmosphere at ComNav. It's more laid back than most jobs I've had. We all get along well and work well together. It's like a big family. Some companies are always looking over your shoulder, but at ComNav, if you're doing your job and getting the work done, no one will stand over you and make you feel uncomfortable. Marty gives us less stress by giving us more freedom. Another of Marty's favorite phrases is "How does it affect me?" If our job is less stressful, he has happy employees. Happy employees work hard. Hard working employees make more money. With that said, every few months Marty throws a company party or he may buy us all pizza for lunch. When he throws a company party we shut down at noon and he pays us for the whole day. He pays us to have fun! We sit back and relax. Employees bring outdoor games to play. Our families are invited and the stress-relieving begins.

It's always a good time for everyone. Marty's pretty laid back most of the time and more than willing to help you out on anything you need. People here are very loyal. That's the family mindset we have here. Marty is always thinking of everyone's mental welfare. The ComNav equation is: Happy employees equal happy customers. Very few employers accommodate people as much as ComNav does. It seems to me once you get hired and you work hard, you'll be here forever unless you do something really terrible.

ComNav is by far the best company I've ever worked for. Marty is a great person to work for, and he is truly a legend in his own mind. (But don't tell him I said so.)

Scott Pusey
Vice President, Sales and Marketing, Eight years

One of my earliest memories of ComNav was during a Bridge Crew Meeting. The purpose of that meeting is to have a roundtable discussion with people representing engineering, sales, accounting and production. It was during this meeting the accounting person was asked about accounts receivable and she stated she might not be able to make payroll that week. Huh? I remained silent until after the meeting broke up. I felt the need to speak to Marty about this since I had relocated from Maryland just two weeks prior. "Did I hear correctly?" I asked him. He said, "Yep. I told you we weren't in the best financial shape." Yet with all the team pulling together, we were able to right the ship and within two years the company had become profitable to the point where we had our payables under control and actually started the profit-sharing with our employees.

I worked for a couple of our competitors in sales about 12 years. ComNav is smaller and the desire here for growth is different. As the only sales person at this company, I have more of a responsibility to make sure everyone here has work. Eight years ago when I came to work here, there were eight employees. Now there are 40. We all benefit by the growth we've experienced. Larger companies have larger inside sales forces. Here it's just me and I enjoy that. I wake up every day wanting to come to work. In my contract I'm responsible for the entire universe. We do have foreign sales, but not that foreign! I have external sales reps who sell our product and complimenting products. They get more than the average percentage for their sales and we give them outstanding support. Our success comes from the entire team. It's the communication with the customers and the quality of our work that has earned us the success we enjoy.

We enjoy a profit-sharing plan here. The more we grow, he more our stock price grows. Today the price per share has increased by over 7,000% from what it was when I joined the company. (That's *not* a typo!)

Beth Burrill
Human Resources and Accounting, 12 years

Though my background was in business management and customer service, I was ready for a change of pace and started at ComNav as an assembler. The interest I had for arts and crafts made me think I'd like building things on an assembly line. After eight months I began working for the CFO and am now known as the company's Bean Countess. Even though debits and credits are not my personal bliss, I love my job here. It allows me a work schedule that works for my family and I'm very grateful.

The people here are invested in each other and in the success of the company. Marty calls us the island of misfit toys. It fits us. He comes from the school of thought where a handshake means something. Though he jokingly states, "How does it affect me?" He's very selfless and has taken personal risks to keep the company and its people afloat numerous times. He is very big on family and that is what we all are to each other.

Even though he is my boss, I am fearless to tell him what I think he needs to hear. I think the freedom to be so honest really works for both of us even though we are as opposite as a conservative and a liberal can be.

Jeff Denyer
Mechanical Guru, 13 years

Before I began working at this company I was a cook at a local restaurant in Freeport. In 1994 I began doing refrigeration and air-conditioning repair to supplement my income from the very seasonal restaurant business, and was quite successful with this. My father owned a machine shop and I got to play around in it a lot when I was a kid and learned a lot about the trade.

I was hired in 1999 as a surface grinder operator at ComNav Engineering. This was a great opportunity for me as I have always been mechanically inclined. I was in the machine shop for a little over a year when a position opened up as an inventory manager. Being in this new position allowed me to learn a lot about how our product is made as well as how it is designed.

In 2008 Marty decided that we needed to be able to do more of our own machining in-house and the decision was made to expand our metal working shop. Marty purchased our first CNC machining center which gave us the new capability of machining our own cavity filters in-house. After a brief training they turned me loose and I started machining cavity filters. Around 2010 Marty added a CNC turning center in order to expand our machining capabilities even more. I currently live in Bath with my wife and son and commute to Portland. There are several reasons why I really like working at ComNav. The benefit package is unbeatable, the atmosphere is relaxed and casual, and the people are more like family than coworkers. Several times a year the company does a party or outing and we all have a great time. When we have an issue, everyone comes together to make it work. There's a terrific spirit of cooperation from Marty all the way down to the newest hire.

11 The Bottom Line

The Plan

The key to starting any enterprise is to actually sit down and write a business plan. It focuses your thoughts, helps you think through all the details, and becomes your operations manual to get through the start-up phase. It is also your main selling tool when talking to banks and potential investors. They will want to know if you have really thought it through and, above all, how they will get their money back. Writing a business plan is a difficult and time-consuming task but it is an extremely valuable asset in getting people to actually take you seriously. You cannot go to a bank or investor and just say you have an idea for a business. If you do they will laugh you out of the office.

A well-written business plan will contain a financing strategy, a marketing strategy, an operational plan, target customers, a description of your product, sales forecasts and financial forecasts. It is basically a book of dreams and is almost completely void of any actual facts. It is your prediction of the future based on assumptions, estimates, hopes and desires. As I said in the beginning, it is total unadulterated bullshit, a big steaming pile of manure. But it is your pile and you believe it. Now you must get other people to believe. Actually if it's a good plan, with a good business model, in a good market, it is not that hard to get people to believe it. People with money are looking for businesses in which to invest. You just need to find the right person with the right personality and the ability to understand your market and your product. Luckily for me I found my partner, Lee.

In the words of Erwin Rommel, "Every plan is good

until the first shot is fired." You must be flexible and make changes and adjustments as conditions change (and they will). This is the key to entramanureship: You have to be able to adjust to the crap that is thrown at you every day. Customers will come and go; key people will come and go; markets crash; terrorists crash planes into buildings, all kinds of events both internal and external beyond your control can drastically affect your company for good or bad. The only real thing you can consistently expect is inconsistency. So you must remain flexible and adapt to any situation as it presents itself.

Manure is an excellent metaphor for the systems, processes, and people you put in place to fertilize and grow your company. In addition to nutrients, manure provides carbon and other constituents that affect the soil's moisture content, biological activity and physical structure.

Bottom Line: Everything that happens in the line of doing business, whether perceived as good or bad, ultimately develops the character (ethos) of the company.

Manure Has Several Effects on the Soil System

Manure is an invaluable way to improve soil, but it can be a major pollultant if you do not pay attention to how it works in the soil.

Bottom Line: Your people work in your soil. How they work in your particular soil determines the efficiency and effectiveness of your ability to achieve your goals.

Most people will rise to the occasion, take on their responsibilities and excel when given the freedom and flexibility to own their jobs. Every single person in your organization contributes to your success (or detracts from it).

Occasionally you will make a bad hire and this individual

will turn out to be a major pollutant in your soil. You must recognize it as soon as possible and move that person out of your organization quickly. This is not easy. People have a way of covering their trails, setting up smoke screens and misdirecting attention elsewhere. But usually the situation will become apparent in a short time. I hate to fire people; it makes me feel like a failure, and putting it off only makes the situation worse. Once you make the decision that it needs to be done, don't wait until Friday, or think about it over the weekend. Just do it. It's like pulling off a Band-Aid. It hurts for a minute and once it's done you end up with a sense of relief. There are occasions where you do not hate firing someone, but you still feel a sense of failure for hiring him or her in the first place. If someone is doctoring the time clock, embezzling, maliciously hurting the company in some way, or out and out dishonest, that individual is definitely a pollutant and must be removed immediately.

Then there is the case of over-fertilization. Layoffs are the absolute worst. These people did nothing wrong, but you need to right-size to save your company. It's similar to an animal caught in a trap that chews off a limb to survive. You feel a devastating sense of failure. These people counted on you for their living and you let them down. It takes weeks to recover from a layoff. Not to mention that the people left are wondering if they are next at any minute. So be careful not to over-fertilize. It is better to have people working lots of overtime than to have people trying to find work to do.

Immediate Supply of Nutrients

Manure contains nitrogen (as ammonium), phosphorus, potassium, and micronutrients that can be used directly by plants. This is the most recognized value of manure.

Bottom Line: The systems you put in place, the way you conduct business, your quality system, purchasing system and operations procedures all provide the framework around which your organization grows and thrives. Like the framing in a tomato patch or a vineyard, they provide the structure in which your fertilized garden grows. The manure you apply when creating this framework are the databases, work orders and procedures. At the beginning it is all hypothetical. You believe in your heart that these frameworks will create an efficiently operating organization. You know it is more bullshit, but you are hoping over time you will recognize the weaknesses and tweak the infrastructure for better efficiencies. Hey, you have to start somewhere and if you are starting from nothing, all you have to work with is your past experiences and guesswork.

Delayed Supply of Nutrients

Other nutrients in manure are part of organic (carbon-containing) compounds. These compounds trigger biological activity that makes nutrients in the manure and other organic matter available to plants.

Bottom Line: Success doesn't happen overnight. You plant a seed; you give it nutrients; you wait. Eventually it happens. From your initial setup of the company's operations, to your first hire, to your marketing strategy, you never know at the beginning if you have the right mix of nutrients to make your company grow. It takes patience and determination and a steady focus to keep everything on track. As you grow you make subtle changes and remix your initial batch of manure and adapt as the ground of your business environment changes.

Salt and Ammonia Toxicity

Manure contains high levels of salts that burn leaves when applied to growing plants. High levels of ammonia or ammonium in fresh manure can hinder seed germination.

Bottom Line: Entremanureship requires you to be ever mindful of potential trouble spots. Ferret them out and deal with them before they ruin the entire crop. Learn from your mistakes and let them go. Don't keep trying to push a bad idea, no matter how much you have invested in it. Whether it is financial, physical, or mental capital, it's already spent and it's not coming back. Don't let it influence the options you must take to correct the problem and move on.

The concept of sunk cost is very difficult to embrace but you must. Don't constrain your future with your past. That would be a mistake.

Improved Soil Structure

The increased biological activity and organic matter improve the soil structure by binding soil into aggregates. In the words of S.W. Fletcher in 1910, "When incorporated with the soil, [manure] greatly improves the texture, loosening a heavy compact soil and binding together a light leachy one; making the soil more friable, warmer, more retentive of moisture and more congenial to plants in every way." (S.W. Fletcher, 1910. Soils: How to Handle and Improve Them, Garden City Doubleday, Page & Company, p. 348.)

Bottom Line: As your company matures, your people will mature in their jobs and work more cohesively together. Strengths and weaknesses will become apparent and certain people will gravitate towards their strengths and away from their weaknesses. Let this happen naturally and don't try to force square pegs into round holes. If individuals hate certain tasks, there is usually someone else who doesn't mind doing them. If people like their jobs they will be efficient at them. If not, they will constantly make mistakes and develop bad attitudes. There are always jobs and tasks that nobody likes, so spread it around and rotate it so no one person gets stuck with it and ends up feeling picked upon.

Enhanced Biological Activity

Manure affects the mix of organisms in soil, but these changes are poorly studied. Manure may affect pest and nutrient cycles by changing the diversity of soil organisms that compete with pests and that transform plant nutrients.

Bottom Line: Be open to new ideas and ways of improving your operation. Change is not always bad. Change usually works best from the bottom up rather than the top down. If an employee discovers a new, better way of doing something, take it seriously. There may be unintended consequences downstream in the process but look at the idea and investigate it. If it works, reward the employee for coming up with it. We do this with the Crapper Award. Employees love the recognition and it proves to them that they are a valuable part of the company. Issuing edicts from above rarely works and before long people will drift back to what they were doing before.

Don't be overly concerned when something happens that seems bad. Your company just might be better off after you go through the crisis. Crisis moments are usually a wake-up call. You have become sloppy; an external force rattled your company; a competitor sniped a big customer, or you experience a design flaw. Any number of things could send a company into crisis. It is how you deal with it that counts. Adapt to the new environment, implement stronger process controls, do additional employee training: Any number of solutions will present themselves. In the end the company will usually emerge stronger, healthier and more efficient. An occasional crisis is actually a good thing. It doesn't seem so when you are in the middle of it, but when it's over you will recognize the teaching moment. No matter how bad things look today, there is always tomorrow. Things can get better just as fast as they turned bad.

Different Animal Species Produce Different Types of Manure

A ton of fresh manure from most species contains about 10 to 20 pounds of nitrogen, 5 to 10 pounds of phosphorus, and 10 to 15 pounds of potassium. However, nitrogen and phosphorus levels are even higher in poultry manure, and sheep manure contains greater potassium levels.

Bottom Line: Every person in your organization has a talent or skill or ability that (when amalgamated with the others), enhances your ability to achieve success. No one individual is more important to the success of the organization than any other, including you. I can do pretty much anybody's job in the company, but not all the jobs in the company at the same time. In addition I am not anywhere near as good as they are at their jobs. Saying I can do it is one thing; doing it well is something altogether different.

The hardest thing to fight in any organization is the Us-versus-Them attitude between managers and staff. You need direct lines of responsibility, but it must be done with open lines of communication. I try to maintain as flat an organization as possible. There are only three layers on our organizational chart: myself, my immediate staff, and everyone else. Anybody can (and does) walk into my office with any problem, whether it is job-related, political or personal.

Another key point: I have found that it never works to share people. People need to have one and only one supervisor. Otherwise confusion will reign and the individual will not know exactly what is expected and will do whatever the last person he or she talked to said to do. Priorities get thrown out the window. Every individual provides a different portion to the mix. No contribution is too small or you wouldn't be doing it in the first place. It takes all kinds of people of various skills and attitudes to maintain a successful organization. Entremanures need them all!

Retrospective

After 16 years my pile of manure has fertilized a growing thriving enterprise with contented employees, happy investors, satisfied customers, and I made a few bucks along the way. The company currently is almost nothing like what I described in my original business plan. It is better in most ways and worse in a few. I have different customers, an expanded market niche, an expanded product line, different manufacturing processes, and a different organization chart. All of these changes are the result of adapting to a changing environment.

When I look back at where I came from (the stoner kid in high school, flunking out of my first attempt at college, my time in the Navy, late nights studying in engineering school), I can only look back and think *WOW*. All of the seemingly disconnected events in my past led me down the road to where I am now. It has been a long road and I wouldn't change a thing. Even the bad stuff with the company's almost dying several times has given me a perspective: No matter how dark it gets, there is always tomorrow.

If you really pay attention to all that life throws at you, you realize that, fail or succeed, you never give up. You never dismiss an experience, but rather embrace it and turn it into the next one around the corner. You take what you've been exposed to and use it to your advantage, turning it into something that takes you to the next step. Then one day you wake up and realize, "I did it!"

Bottom Line:
Now keep it going.

www.ingramcontent.com/pod-product-compliance
Lightning Source LLC
Chambersburg PA
CBHW061512180526
45171CB00001B/141